Pocket
PRAGUE
TOP SIGHTS • LOCAL LIFE • MADE EASY

Mark Baker

In This Book

QuickStart Guide

Your keys to understanding the city – we help you decide what to do and how to do it

Need to Know
Tips for a smooth trip

Neighbourhoods
What's where

Explore Prague

The best things to see and do, neighbourhood by neighbourhood

Top Sights
Make the most of your visit

Local Life
The insider's city

The Best of Prague

The city's highlights in handy lists to help you plan

Best Walks
See the city on foot

Prague's Best...
The best experiences

Survival Guide

Tips and tricks for a seamless, hassle-free city experience

Getting Around
Travel like a local

Essential Information
Including where to stay

Our selection of the city's best places to eat, drink and experience:

◉ **Sights**

✖ **Eating**

🍷 **Drinking**

✪ **Entertainment**

🔒 **Shopping**

These symbols give you the vital information for each listing:

📞 Telephone Numbers	🚌 Bus
⊘ Opening Hours	🚤 Ferry
🅿 Parking	Ⓜ Metro
⊘ Nonsmoking	Ⓢ Subway
@ Internet Access	🚋 Tram
🛜 Wi-Fi Access	🚆 Train
🥗 Vegetarian Selection	
👪 Family-Friendly	

Find each listing quickly on maps for each neighbourhood:

Bar Hemingway

16 🍷 Map p233, B2

Legend has it that Hem self, wielding a machine rate this timber-pan ered bar during showpiece is a en by Papa an town. Dress s.com; Hôtel Rit ⊘6.30pm-2a

Lonely Planet's Prague

Lonely Planet Pocket Guides are designed to get you straight to the heart of the city.

Inside you'll find all the must-see sights, plus tips to make your visit to each one really memorable. We've split the city into easy-to-navigate neighbourhoods and provided clear maps so you'll find your way around with ease. Our expert authors have searched out the best of the city: walks, food, nightlife and shopping, to name a few. Because you want to explore, our 'Local Life' pages will take you to some of the most exciting areas to experience the real Prague.

And of course you'll find all the practical tips you need for a smooth trip: itineraries for short visits, how to get around, and how much to tip the guy who serves you a drink at the end of a long day's exploration.

It's your guarantee of a really great experience.

Our Promise

You can trust our travel information because Lonely Planet authors visit the places we write about, each and every edition. We never accept freebies for positive coverage, so you can rely on us to tell it like it is.

QuickStart Guide 7

Explore Prague 21

Worth a Trip:

The Best of Prague 135

Prague's Best Walks

Prague's Best...

Survival Guide 159

QuickStart Guide

Welcome to Prague

More than 20 years after the Velvet Revolution drew back the curtain on this intoxicating maze of winding cobble-stone alleyways, the 'city of a hundred spires' thrills visitors with dramatic Gothic architecture, down-to-earth pubs, ornate cafes, cutting-edge art and the grand Prague Castle, looming high over the city and looking as if straight out of a fairy tale.

View from Old Town Bridge Tower (p77)
SYLVAIN SONNET/GETTY IMAGES ©

Prague Top Sights

Prague Castle (p24)

Looming high above the Vltava's western bank, this outrageously outsized fortress conjures up childhood fairy tales of a good king watching benevolently over his people.

VISIONS OF OUR LAND/GETTY IMAGES ©

St Vitus Cathedral (p30)

The Gothic centrepiece of Prague Castle is famous for its beautiful stained- and painted-glass windows, ornate chapels, and spires that seem to pierce the sky.

Old Town Square & Astronomical Clock (p74)

The spooky (at night, at least) Gothic spires of the Church of Our Lady Before Týn rise above this famous square, known in part for its Astronomical Clock, where every hour, 'Death' rings a bell and inverts his hourglass.

Charles Bridge (p76)

This stunning stone bridge, commissioned by Emperor Charles IV in 1357 and lined with saintly statues, provides an unforgettable passage between the Old Town and Malá Strana.

Jewish Museum (p60)

This extensive museum is spread out over six important sites in Prague's former Jewish quarter, including the beautiful Spanish Synagogue.

Old Jewish Cemetery (p62)

With 12,000 gravestones and several tens of thousands of additional bodies packed into a space the size of a few suburban gardens, Prague's Old Jewish Cemetery is like no other on earth.

Loreta (p32)

A baroque place of pilgrimage, the Loreta is noted for its cloister and chapels, a lavish, diamond-studded artwork, and the ancient bells that ring out over the city of Prague from its clock tower. And a bearded lady.

Petřín Hill (p42)

The 318m-high grassy knoll, popular with joggers, dog-walkers, lovers and families, offers magnificent vistas across the city of a hundred spires. Take the funicular up here, just like they did for the 1891 Prague Jubilee.

Wenceslas Square (p92)

Pictured on postcards that highlight the equestrian statue of 'Good King Wenceslas', the massive square was once a gathering point for proud Czechs and Velvet Revolution demonstrators.

Veletržní Palác (p126)

Well off the tourist trail in Holešovice, this larger-than-life functionalist structure houses an impressive collection of avant-garde Czech art and works by European masters such as Cézanne, Rodin, Klimt and Schiele. It also has Mucha's oversized *Slav Epic*.

Prague Local Life

Insider tips to help you find the real city

Czechs are a cool, laid-back bunch fond of walking their dogs down to the beer garden. After you've seen the castle and walked across Charles Bridge, join the locals in their favourite parks, residential neighbourhoods and watering holes.

Gardens of Malá Strana (p44)

▶ Gardens Beneath Prague Castle
▶ Wallenstein Garden

In the shadows of Prague Castle, the city's 'Lesser Quarter' has a particularly high concentration of lovely parks and gardens. Do as the locals do and seek refuge in the green spaces: bring a blanket, a book and a beer to one of these inviting urban oases.

Drinking in Vinohrady & Žižkov (p114)

▶ Riegrovy Sady Beer Garden
▶ Bukowski's

Žižkov's proud citizens claim their neighbourhood has more pubs per square metre than anywhere else in the world. Neighbouring Vinohrady is filled with fashionable cocktail lounges and wine bars. Put them together and you've got a great boozy night out on the town.

Vyšehrad, Prague's Other Castle (p110)

▶ Vyšehrad Cemetery
▶ Church of Sts Peter & Paul

Prague's 'second' castle is very different from its first, but equally dramatic in its own right. Indeed, it's been centuries since any real castle stood here, but this ruined citadel more than atones for its architectural shortcomings with breathtaking views of the Vltava River and up to Prague Castle.

Beer & Culture in Smíchov (p56)

▶ Zlatý klas
▶ Meet Factory

Though it's slowly gentrifying, this industrial neighbourhood is still known for its edgy, alternative art scene, down-to-earth bars and good theatre. It's close to the centre, but just far enough off the beaten path to allow visitors a taste of the 'real' Prague.

Radost FX (p123), Vinohrady

Vyšehrad Citadel (p110)

LONELY PLANET/GETTY IMAGES ©

RICHARD NEBESKY/GETTY IMAGES ©

Other places to experience the city like a local:

Tankovna pubs (p67)

Kavárna Velryba (p108)

Kampa Island (p48)

Riegrovy sady (p121)

DOX Centre for Contemporary Art (p132)

Stromovka Park (p129)

Lehká Hlava (p82)

Prague Day Planner

Day One

Just one day in Prague? Focus on major sights. Start early, joining the crowd below the **Astronomical Clock** (p75) for the hourly chiming, then wander through **Old Town Square** (p74), taking in the spectacular array of architectural styles and the spires of the **Church of Our Lady Before Týn** (p75). Stop for coffee and a bite at charming **Bakeshop Praha** (p65) before a short stroll through **Josefov** (p58), the former Jewish ghetto. You won't have time to see the **Jewish Museum** (p60), but a walk will give you the feel.

Amble through the winding alleys of the Old Town on your way to one of Prague's most famous landmarks, **Charles Bridge** (p76). While crossing the statue-bedecked bridge, stop to take photos of the Vltava River, with magnificent **Prague Castle** (p24) looming high over the fairy-tale scene. Hike up to the castle along **Nerudova** (p49) through Malá Strana and spend the afternoon visiting **St Vitus Cathedral** (p96) and the castle's formal gardens and exhibits.

For dinner, treat yourself to a meal with a view at **Villa Richter** (p36), just near the castle, or walk back down to Malá Strana for upscale Czech food at **Elegantes** (p50).

Day Two

Spend the morning exploring the quaint backstreets and the **Kampa gardens** (p45) of Malá Strana, one of the city's oldest districts. Catch the **Petřín Funicular** (p43) to enjoy sweeping views from the **Lookout Tower** (p43) at the top of Petřín. From here, find the serene path that crosses over to the **Strahov Monastery** (p35), and then head downhill along **Nerudova** (p49), stopping into elegant **Wallenstein Garden** (p45) at the bottom. Laugh at the **Proudy** (p45) sculpture before treating yourself to a late lunch at the lovely riverside restaurant **Hergetova Cihelna** (p50).

Cross the river via Mánes Bridge. In the afternoon, check out the famous synagogues of the **Jewish Museum** (p60), and then take a break with coffee and cake on the balcony of the striking, cubist **Grand Cafe Orient** (p84).

Stop by the box office of the **National Theatre** (p107) to see if any last-minute tickets are available to the opera or ballet. Before the show, have a light meal at **Cafe Louvre** (p106). Afterwards, go for a classy nightcap at **Hemingway Bar** (p84) or **Tretter's New York Bar** (p67).

Short on time?
We've arranged Prague's must-sees into these day-by-day itineraries to make sure you see the very best of the city in the time you have available.

Day Three

Start with coffee at **Kavárna Slavia** (p106), choosing a table at the front looking out to Prague Castle. Amble over to **Slav Island** (p105) and rent a paddleboat to splash about in the river before heading south to see the **Dancing Building** (p105). From here, walk back up Národní třída to **Wenceslas Square** (p92), taking time to see the nearby sights, including the **National Museum** (p95), the **Jan Palach Memorial** (p93) and the **St Wenceslas Statue** (p93). Plan lunch at **Room** (p97), for tapas, or **Jáma** (p99), for beer and burgers.

From here it's an easy metro jaunt to Vyšehrad and the **Vyšehrad Citadel** (p110), where you can wander around the ruins and visit the graves of Dvořák and Mucha in the **cemetery** (p111).

Head back towards town and spend the evening in Vinohrady and Žižkov, choosing one of the area's excellent restaurants, like **Aromi** (p120) or **Bisos** (p120) – or simply go for a beer at the **Riegrovy Sady Beer Garden** (p121).

Day Four

It's time to see a different part of Prague. Start on Old Town Square and walk down elegant Pařížská, before crossing Čech Bridge (Čechův most) and making the climb to **Letná Gardens** (p129). Admire the views from the top, and then make your way east to the **Letná Beer Garden** (p130), if it's too early for beer, make a note to come back.

It's a short walk to the **National Technical Museum** (p129) – perfect if you've got kids. Have lunch at nearby **Peperoncino** (p130), then visit Prague's best (and most underrated) art museum, **Veletržní Palác** (p126). If you've still got some energy (and daylight), stroll through **Stromovka Park** (p129) and enjoy Prague's prettiest piece of green.

Head back toward the Letná Beer Garden to relax with a Gambrinus, then make your way back down towards town. Enjoy a meal at high-end **Kalina** (p81), then go for jazz at a nearby club like **Reduta** (p107) or the **AghaRTA Jazz Centrum** (86). For a quieter option, head for the rooftop terrace **U Prince** (p81) to lift a glass to this lovely city on your last night here.

Need to Know

For more information,
see Survival Guide (p160).

Currency
Czech crown (Koruna česká; Kč)

Language
Czech

Visas
Generally not required for stays of up to
three months.

Money
ATMs are widely available and credit cards
are accepted at many restaurants and
hotels across the city.

Mobile Phones
The Czech Republic uses GSM 900,
compatible with mobile phones from
the rest of Europe, Australia and New
Zealand (but not with most North American
phones).

Time
Central European Time (GMT plus one hour)

Plugs & Adaptors
Most plugs have two round pins; electrical
current is 230V. North American travellers
will need adaptors and, depending on the
device, transformers.

Tipping
It's standard practice in pubs, cafes and
restaurants to add 10% if service has been
good. In a taxi, round up the fare.

1 Before You Go

Your Daily Budget

Budget less than €80
▶ Dorm beds €10–€20
▶ Excellent supermarkets for self-catering
▶ Cheap theatre tickets start at just €4

Midrange €80–€150
▶ Double room at boutique hotel €80–€100
▶ Dinner with local beer/wine €30–€40

Top end more than €150
▶ Double room or suite at luxury hotel
€120–€200
▶ Four-course dinner at top restaurants €80

Useful Websites

▶ **Lonely Planet** (www.lonelyplanet.com/
czech-republic/prague) Destination info, hotel
bookings, traveller forum and more.

▶ **Prague City Tourism** (www.prague.eu)
Prague's official tourism portal.

▶ **Prague.com** (www.prague.com) A city
guide plus hotel bookings.

▶ **Prague Public Transit** (www.dpp.cz)
Handy journey planner for all public transport, with an excellent English-language
section.

Advance Planning

One month before Reserve your hotel room,
especially for smaller B&Bs or boutique
hotels.

Two weeks before Check performance-
venue websites and order tickets for shows.

One day before Check the Prague Castle
website (www.hrad.cz) to find out about
the next day's cultural events.

② Arriving in Prague

Public transport and private taxis are easily available from both main arrival hubs.

✈ From Václav Havel Airport Prague

Destination	Best Transport
Old Town	Cedaz shuttle bus to náměstí Republiky
Malá Strana & Hradčany	Taxi or bus 119 to metro station Dejvická, connection to Malostranská metro station (plus tram for Hradčany)
Wenceslas Square	Airport Express (AE) bus to Hlavní Nádraží train station area
Vinohrady & Žižkov	Taxi or bus 119 to metro station Dejvická, connection to Náměstí Miru or Jiřího z Poděbrad metro station

🚊 From Praha Hlavní Nádraží (Prague Main Train Station)

Destination	Best Transport
Old Town	Metro Line C to Muzeum, transfer to Line A to Staroměstská station
Malá Strana & Hradčany	Metro Line C to Muzeum, transfer to Line A to Malostranská station (plus tram for Hradčany)
Wenceslas Square	Walk (it's two blocks away)
Vinohrady & Žižkov	Metro Line C to Muzeum, transfer to Line A to Náměstí Miru or Jiřího z Poděbrad metro station

③ Getting Around

Prague's public transport system is affordable and efficient, and one of Europe's best. Most visitors will get everywhere they need to go by walking, taking the metro or hopping on a tram.

Ⓜ Metro

Prague's metro system runs from 5am to midnight, with fast, frequent service. For tourists, the most useful line is A (green), which runs from Dejvická (airport connection) to Prague Castle, Malá Strana, Old Town Square, Wenceslas Square and Vinohrady.

🚋 Tram

Travelling on the trams in Prague is part of the cultural experience. Regular trams run from 5am to midnight. Important lines to remember are 22 (runs to Prague Castle, Malá Strana and Charles Bridge, Nové Město, and Vinohrady), 17 and 18 (run to the Jewish Quarter and Old Town Square), and 11 (runs to Žižkov and Vinohrady). After midnight, night trams (51 to 58) rumble across the city about every 40 minutes.

🚕 Taxi

Taxis are a convenient option when you're in a hurry, but be careful of scams. Look for the 'Taxi Fair Place' stations in key tourist areas: drivers can charge a maximum fare and must announce the estimated price in advance. Make sure you know the current exchange rate if the driver offers you the chance to pay in a foreign currency.

Prague Neighbourhoods

Prague Castle & Hradčany (p22)
This refined hilltop district is defined by the massive castle complex that gives Prague its dreamy, fairy-tale-like appearance.

◉ Top Sights

Prague Castle

St Vitus Cathedral

Loreta

Jewish Museum & Josefov (p58)
Today, Prague's one-time Jewish ghetto is home to a cluster of historic synagogues and the eerie but beautiful Old Jewish Cemetery.

◉ Top Sights

Jewish Museum

Old Jewish Cemetery

Malá Strana & Petřín Hill (p40)
Quaint, cobblestoned streets, red roofs, ancient cloisters and a peaceful hillside park characterise Prague's charming 'Lesser Quarter'.

◉ Top Sights

Petřín Hill

Old Town Square & Staré Město (p72)
Gothic spires, art nouveau architecture, a quirky astronomical clock and horse-drawn carriages crowd this colourful, famous old square.

◉ Top Sights

Old Town Square & Astronomical Clock

Charles Bridge

Wenceslas Square & Around (p90)
Once a horse market, this huge square has been the site of many important moments in Czech history.

◉ Top Sights

Wenceslas Square

St Vitus Cathedral

Prague Castle

Loreta

Old Jewish Cemetery

Jewish Museum

Charles Bridge

Old Town Square & Astronomical Clock

Petřín Hill

Holešovice (p124)
Beer gardens, contemporary art and huge parks characterise this laid-back district that's well off the tourist path.

◉ Top Sights

Veletržní Palác

◉
Veletržní Palác

◉
Wenceslas Square

Nové Město (p102)
Cool modern architecture and quiet riverside cafes are the crowning glories of this underrated neighbourhood.

Vinohrady & Žižkov (p112)
The locals' residential neighbourhood of choice, this leafy area contains many of Prague's hippest bars and cafes.

Explore
Prague

Worth a Trip

Charles Bridge (p76) and Old Town
IMAGES BY FABIO/GETTY IMAGES ©

Explore

Prague Castle & Hradčany

The spires of St Vitus Cathedral, rising up from the heart of Prague Castle, are rarely out of view when you're wandering around the city. In Hradčany (the castle district), visitors are particularly conscious of the royal omnipresence; passing through the doll-sized alleyways, you'll have an idea what life was like for the castle's hard-working medieval minions.

MATTHEW DIXON/GETTY IMAGES ©

The Sights in a Day

Get an early start for your assault on **Prague Castle** (p24). Eat breakfast and have coffee beforehand, since there aren't many early-morning options up here. Buy an admission ticket at the information centre and head straight for **St Vitus Cathedral** (p30) to check out the magnificent church before the crowds show up. Visit the **Old Royal Palace** (p25) and **Golden Lane** (p27) before taking a break in the **Royal Garden** (p29). Make your way back to the castle entrance for the changing of the guard at noon.

After lunch, walk down to the **Loreta** (p32) and take the audio tour of the major sights, including **Santa Casa** (p33) and the **Church of the Nativity of Our Lord** (p33). Spend the rest of the afternoon perusing the National Gallery's fine holdings of European art at **Šternberg Palace** (p36) or the Theology and Philosophy halls of the nearly thousand-year-old **Strahov Monastery** (p35). Check out the nearby quirky **Miniature Museum** (p35).

Hradčany is quiet at night, but you can pair a late-afternoon stroll through the Nový Svět quarter with a romantic dinner at **U Zlaté Hrušky** (p36), or have something even more elegant at **Villa Richter** (p36).

 Top Sights

Prague Castle (p24)

St Vitus Cathedral (p30)

Loreta (p32)

 Best of Prague

Food

U zlaté hrušky (p36)

Villa Richter (p36)

Lobkowicz Palace Café (p36)

Art

Prague Castle Picture Gallery (p25)

Šternberg Palace (p36)

Stained-glass windows of St Vitus Cathedral (p30)

For Free

Prague Castle (p24)

Getting There

🅼 **Metro** Take Line A to Malostranská, then climb the steps.

🚊 **Tram** Take 22 to Pražský hrad then walk five minutes, or to Pohořelec then walk downhill.

Top Sights
Prague Castle

Known simply as *hrad* (castle) to proud Praguers, Prague Castle was founded by 9th-century Přemysl princes and grew haphazardly as subsequent rulers built additions. Today, it's a huge complex, larger than seven football fields, proceeding west to east through a series of three courtyards. There have been four major reconstructions. Many Czech rulers have resided here; one notable exception is the first postcommunist president, Václav Havel: in 1989, he plumped for the comforts of his own home instead.

◉ Map p34, D2

www.hrad.cz

adult/concession short tour 250/125Kc, long tour 350/175Kc

🕓9am-5pm Apr-Oct, to 4pm Nov-Mar

🚊22, Ⓜ Malostranská

Prague Castle and Vltava River

Don't Miss

Castle Entrance

The castle's main gate, on Hradčany Square, is flanked by huge, 18th-century statues of battling Titans that dwarf the castle guards below. Playwright-turned-president Václav Havel hired the Czech costume designer on the film *Amadeus* to redesign the guards' uniforms and instigated a changing-of-the-guard ceremony – the most impressive display is at noon.

Prague Castle Picture Gallery

In 1648 an invading Swedish army looted Emperor Rudolf II's art collection (as well as making off with the original bronze statues in the Wallenstein Garden). The **gallery** (www.kulturanahrade. cz; adult/child 150/80Kč; ⏰9am-6pm Apr-Oct, to 4pm Nov-Mar) in these converted Renaissance stables houses what was left, as well as replacement works, including some by Rubens, Tintoretto and Titian.

Plečník Monolith

In the third courtyard, a noteworthy feature near St Vitus Cathedral is a huge granite monolith dedicated to the victims of WWI, designed by Slovene architect Jože Plečnik in 1928. Nearby is a copy of the castle's famous statue of St George slaying the dragon.

Old Royal Palace

The palace's highlight is the high-Gothic vaulted roof of **Vladislav Hall** (Vladislavský sál; 1493–1502), beneath which all the presidents of the Czech Republic have been sworn in. There's also a balcony off the hall with great city views and a door to the former Bohemian Chancellery, where the Second Defenestration of Prague occurred in 1618.

☑ Top Tips

▶ The castle buildings open at 9am; be there a few minutes early to beat the crowds.

▶ You'll need at least half a day to explore the castle grounds.

▶ Guided tours of the castle in English can be arranged in advance by calling ☎224 373 584. Tours last around an hour and leave from the information centres.

▶ To catch music and cultural events at the castle grounds, check out www.kulturanahrade. cz for a schedule of events.

✗ Take a Break

There are several places scattered around the castle grounds to stop for a coffee or cold drink. Our favourite – also a good stop for lunch – is the lovely Lobkowicz Palace Café (p36), located on the ground level of Lobkowicz Palace.

Prague Castle

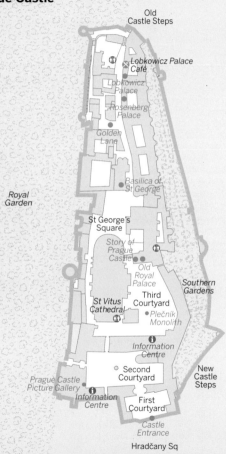

Old
Castle Steps

Lobkowicz Palace
Café

Lobkowicz
Palace

Rosenberg
Palace

Golden
Lane

Basilica of
St George

Royal
Garden

St George's
Square

Story of
Prague
Castle

Old
Royal
Palace

Southern
Gardens

Third
Courtyard

St Vitus
Cathedral

Plečnik
Monolith

Information
Centre

New
Castle
Steps

Second
Courtyard

Prague Castle
Picture Gallery

Information
Centre

First
Courtyard

Castle
Entrance

Hradčany Sq

Golden Lane

Story of Prague Castle

One of the castle's most compelling exhibitions, with an outstanding collection of armour, jewellery, glassware, furniture and other artefacts from more than a thousand years of the castle's history. A particularly memorable sight is the skeleton of the pre-Christian 'warrior', still encased in the earth where archaeologists found him within the castle grounds.

Basilica of St George

Behind a brick-red facade lies the Czech Republic's best-preserved Romanesque church. The original was established in the 10th century by Vratislav I (the father of St Wenceslas), who is still buried here, as is St Ludmilla. It's also popular for small concert performances.

Golden Lane

The tiny, colourful cottages along this cobbled alley, reopened a couple of years ago after extensive renovations, were built in the 16th century for the castle guard's sharpshooters, but were later used by goldsmiths, squatters and artists, including writer Franz Kafka (who stayed at his sister's house at No 22 from 1916 to 1917).

Understand
Kings & Castles

Prague's history, filled with royal betrayals, people tossing each other out of windows, and one man famously being burnt at the stake, makes *The Tudors* look tame by comparison.

In the Beginning
The name 'Bohemia', still used to describe the Czech Republic's western-most province, comes from a Celtic tribe, the Boii, who lived here for centuries before Slavic tribes arrived around the 6th century. Two separate tribes are said to have established themselves, with the 'Czechs' building a wooden fortress near the current Prague Castle, and the Zličani settling at Vyšehrad. The 9th-century Přemysl dynasty built the earliest section of today's Prague Castle in the 9th century, and also included one Václav, or 'Wenceslas', of 'Good King' Christmas-carol fame (see p38).

The Good Times
After the Přemysl dynasty died out, Prague came under the control of the family that eventually produced Holy Roman Emperor Charles IV (1316–78). Under his rule, the city blossomed. Charles – whose mother was Czech – elevated Prague's official status and went on a construction spree, building Nové Město (New Town) and Charles Bridge, founding Charles University and adding St Vitus Cathedral to the castle.

One of the university rectors, Jan Hus, led the 15th-century Hussite movement, which challenged what many saw as the corrupt practices of the Catholic Church. Hus was burnt at the stake at Constance in Germany in 1415 for his reformist 'heresy', but his death kicked off decades of sectarian fighting that eventually put Hussites in charge for several decades.

Habsburg Rule
In 1526 the Czech lands came under the rule of the Austrian Habsburgs. With the Reformation in full swing in Europe, tensions between the Catholic Habsburgs and reformist Czechs inevitably surfaced. In 1618, Bohemian rebels threw two Catholic councillors from a Prague Castle window, sparking the Thirty Years' War (1618–48). Following the defeat of the Czech nobility in 1620 at the Battle of White Mountain (Bílá Hora), Czechs lost their independence to the Habsburgs for 300 years.

Rosenberg Palace

Originally built as the grand residence of the Rosenberg family, this 16th-century Renaissance-style palace was later repurposed by Empress Maria Theresa as a 'Residence for Noblewomen' to house 30 unmarried women at a time. Today, one section of the palace re-creates the style of an 18th-century noblewoman's apartment using artefacts from the Prague Castle's depository.

Lobkowicz Palace

The 16th-century **Lobkowicz Palace** (Lobkovický palác; ☎233 312 925; www. lobkowicz.cz; Jiřská 3; adult/concession/family 275/200/690Kč; ⊙10am-6pm) houses a private museum known as the Princely Collections, with priceless paintings, furniture and musical memorabilia. An included audio guide dictated by owner William Lobkowicz and his family brings the displays to life, making this one of the castle's most interesting attractions.

Royal Garden

Powder Bridge (Prašný most; 1540) spans the **Stag Moat** (Jelení příkop) en route to the spacious Renaissance-style Royal Garden, dating from 1534. The most beautiful building is the **Ball-Game House** (Míčovna; 1569), a masterpiece of Renaissance sgraffito where the Habsburgs once played badminton. East is the **Summer Palace** (Letohrádek; 1538–60) and west the former **Riding School** (Jízdárna; 1695).

Southern Gardens

The three gardens lined up below the castle's southern wall – **Paradise Garden**, the **Hartig Garden** and the **Garden on the Ramparts** – offer superb views over Malá Strana's rooftops. Enter from the west via the New Castle Steps or from the east via the Old Castle Steps.

Top Sights
St Vitus Cathedral

The largest and most noteworthy church in the Czech Republic was begun in 1344. Though it appears Gothic to the tips of its pointy spires, much of St Vitus Cathedral was only completed in time for its belated consecration in 1929. The coronations of Bohemia's kings were held here until the mid-19th century. Today it's the seat of the Archbishop of Prague and the final resting place of some of the nation's most illustrious figures – kings, princes, even saints.

◉ Map p34, D2

www.katedralasvateho-vita.cz

admission incl in Prague Castle tour ticket

🕘9am-5pm Mon-Sat, noon-5pm Sun Apr-Oct, to 4pm Nov-Mar

🚊22

St Vitus Cathedral

Don't Miss

Stained-Glass Windows

The interior is flooded with colour from stained-glass windows created by eminent Czech artists of the early 20th century. In the third chapel on the northern side (to the left as you enter) is one by art nouveau artist Alfons Mucha, depicting the lives of Sts Cyril and Methodius.

Golden Gate

The cathedral's south entrance is known as the Golden Gate (Zlatá brána), an elegant, triple-arched Gothic porch designed by Peter Parler.

Royal Oratory

Kings addressed their subjects from this grand, intricately crafted oratory (1493) that appears to be woven with gnarled tree branches. This striking centrepiece exemplifies late-Gothic aesthetics.

Tomb of St John of Nepomuk

Nepomuk was a priest and a religious martyr; it's said that hundreds of years after his death, when his body was exhumed, his tongue was found 'still alive'. The Church canonised him and commissioned this elaborate silver sarcophagus for his reburial. (Scientists later showed that the 'tongue' was actually brain tissue congealed in blood.)

Chapel of St Wenceslas

The most beautiful of the cathedral's side chapels, with walls adorned with gilded panels containing polished slabs of semiprecious stones. Murals from the early-16th century depict scenes from the life of the Czechs' patron saint, while even older frescos show scenes from the life of Jesus. On the southern side a small door – locked with seven locks – leads to the coronation chamber, where the Bohemian crown jewels (see p38) are kept.

☑ Top Tips

▶ Try to arrive first thing in the morning, when the crowds are smaller.

▶ Entry to the church is no longer free, but included in both short- and long-term Prague Castle combined-entry tickets.

▶ For spectacular views, climb the stairway to the cathedral's tower.

▶ To attend a service here, inquire at the information centres for times.

✗ Take a Break

Before braving the crowds, fortify with a steaming cup of jasmine tea or light meal at Malý Buddha (p37), located outside the castle complex a short walk from the main entrance.

For coffee, beer or lunch, try U Zavěšenýho Kafe (p38). It's also situated outside the castle complex.

Top Sights
Loreta

The Loreta is a baroque place of pilgrimage financed by the noble Lobkowicz family in 1626. It was designed as a replica of the supposed Santa Casa (Sacred House, the home of the Virgin Mary) in the Holy Land. Legend has it that the original Santa Casa was carried by angels to the Italian town of Loreto as the Turks were advancing on Nazareth. The Loreta's original purpose was to wow and woo the local population, and it still manages to dazzle.

 Map p34, B3

www.loreta.cz

adult/concession/family 130/100/270Kč

⌚9am-12.15pm & 1-5pm Apr-Oct, 9.30am-12.15pm & 1-4pm Nov-Mar

🚊22

Loreta

Don't Miss

Santa Casa
The duplicate Santa Casa is in the centre of a courtyard complex, surrounded by cloistered arcades, churches and chapels. The interior is adorned with 17th-century frescos and reliefs depicting the life of the Virgin Mary, and an ornate silver altar with a wooden effigy of Our Lady of Loreto.

Prague Sun
The eye-popping treasury boasts a star attraction – a dazzling object called the 'Prague Sun'. Studded with 6222 diamonds, it was a gift to the Loreta from Countess Ludmila of Kolowrat. In her will she wrote that the piece must be crafted from her personal collection of diamonds – wedding gifts from her third husband.

Church of the Nativity of Our Lord
Behind the Santa Casa is the Church of the Nativity of Our Lord, built in 1737 to a design by Christoph Dientzenhofer. The claustrophobic interior includes two skeletons of the Spanish saints Felicissima and Marcia, dressed in aristocratic clothing with wax masks concealing their skulls.

The Bearded Lady
At the corner of the courtyard is the unusual Chapel of Our Lady of Sorrows, featuring a crucified bearded lady. She was St Starosta, pious daughter of a Portuguese king who promised her to the king of Sicily against her wishes. After a night of tearful prayers she awoke with a beard, the wedding was called off, and her father had her crucified. She was later made patron saint of the needy and the godforsaken.

☑ **Top Tips**

▶ The worthwhile audio guide, available in several languages, costs 150Kč.

▶ Families (two adults and up to five children under 16) can ask for the 270Kč family rate.

▶ If you'd like to take photos (no flash or tripod allowed), ask for a permit (100Kč).

✕ **Take a Break**

For a cold beer, look no further than old-school Czech pub Pivnice U Černého Vola (p38).

For something more substantial like lunch or dinner, try the nearby U Zlaté Hrušky (p36). In summer sit in the garden across the street.

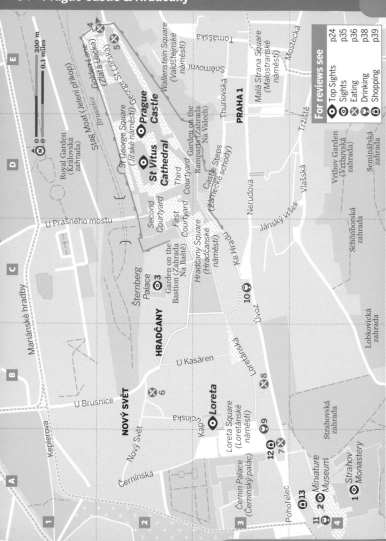

200 m
0.1 miles

Royal Garden (Královská zahrada)

Stag Moat (Jelení příkop)

Brusnice

Golden Lane (Zlatá Ulička)

George St (Jiřská)

Prague Castle

St George Square (Jiřské náměstí)

St Vitus Cathedral

Second Courtyard

Third Courtyard

First Courtyard

Garden on the Ramparts (Zahrada Na Valech)

Castle Steps (Zámecké schody)

Wallenstein Square (Valdštejnské náměstí)

Tomášská

Sněmovní

Thunovská

PRAHA 1

Malá Strana Square (Malostranské náměstí)

Mostecká

U Prašného mostu

Sternberg Palace

Garden on the Bastion (Zahrada Na Baště)

Hradčany Square (Hradčanské náměstí)

Nerudova

Jánský vršek

Vlašská

Tržiště

Seminářská zahrada

Vrtbov Garden (Vrtbovská zahrada)

Schönborská zahrada

Mariánské hradby

HRADČANY

Ke Hradu

U Kasáren

Úvoz

Lobkovická zahrada

Keplerova

U Brusnice

NOVÝ SVĚT

Nový Svět

Kapucínská

Loreta

Loreta Square (Loretánské náměstí)

Loretánská

Strahovská zahrada

Černínská

Černín Palace (Černínský palác)

Pohořelec

Miniature Museum

Strahov Monastery

EDDIE GERALD/ALAMY ©

Miniature Museum

Sights

Strahov Monastery   MONASTERY

1  Map p34, A4

In 1140 Vladislav II founded Strahov Monastery (Strahovský klášter) for the Premonstratensian order. The present monastery buildings, completed in the 17th and 18th centuries, functioned until the communist government closed them down and imprisoned most of the monks; they returned in 1990. (Strahovský klášter; ☎233 107 711; www.strahovskyklaster.cz; Strahovské nádvoří 1; 🚋22)

Miniature Museum   MUSEUM

2  Map p34, A4

Siberian technician Anatoly Konyenko used to manufacture tools for microsurgery, but these days he prefers to spend 7½ years crafting a pair of golden horseshoes for a flea. See those, as well as the Lord's Prayer inscribed on a single human hair, a grasshopper clutching a violin, and a camel caravan silhouetted in the eye of a needle. Weird but fascinating. (Muzeum Miniatur; ☎233 352 371; Strahovské nádvoří II; adult/child 100/50Kč; 🕒9am-5pm; 🚋22)

Top Tip

Visiting Prague Castle

You can purchase two kinds of tickets (each valid for two days) to visit Prague Castle (p24) that allow entry to different combinations of sights. Most short-term visitors opt for the Short Tour:

Short Tour (adult/child/family 250/125/500Kč) – includes St Vitus Cathedral, Old Royal Palace, Basilica of St George, Golden Lane and Daliborka.

Long Tour (adult/child/family 350/175/700Kč) – includes St Vitus Cathedral, Old Royal Palace, Story of Prague Castle, Basilica of St George, Powder Tower, Golden Lane and Daliborka, Prague Castle Picture Gallery, Powder Tower and Rosenberg Palace.

You can buy tickets at either of two information centres in the Second and Third Courtyards.

Šternberg Palace

GALLERY

3 Map p34, C2

The baroque Šternberg Palace is home to the National Gallery's collection of 14th- to 18th-century European art, including works by Goya and Rembrandt. Fans of medieval altarpieces will be in heaven; there are also several Rubens, some Rembrandts and Brueghels, and a large collection of Bohemian miniatures. (Šternberský palác; ☑233 090 570; www.ngprague.cz; Hradčanské náměstí 15; incl admission to Schwarzenberg Palace adult/child 150/80Kč; ☺10am-6pm Tue-Sun; ☒22)

Eating

Villa Richter

CZECH, FRENCH €€

4 Map p34, E2

Housed in a restored 18th-century villa in the middle of a replanted medieval vineyard, this place is aimed squarely at the hordes of tourists thronging up and down the Old Castle Steps. But the setting is special – outdoor tables on terraces with one of the finest views in the city – and the menu of classic Czech dishes doesn't disappoint. (☑257 219 079; www.villarichter.cz; Staré zamecké schody 6; mains 150-300Kč, 3-course dinner 945Kč; ☺11am-11pm; ⓜMalostranská)

Lobkowicz Palace Café

CAFE €€

5 Map p34, E2

This cafe, housed in the 16th-century Lobkowicz Palace, is the best eatery in the castle complex by an imperial mile. Try to grab one of the tables on the balconies at the back – the view over Malá Strana is superb, as is the goulash. The coffee is good too, and service is fast and friendly. (☑233 312 925; Jiřská 3; mains 200-300Kč; ☺10am-6pm; ☎❖; ☒22)

U Zlaté Hrušky

CZECH €€€

6 Map p34, B2

'At the Golden Pear' is a cosy, wood-panelled gourmets' corner, serving Bohemian fish, fowl and game dishes (tripe fricassee is a speciality). It's frequented by locals and visiting dignitaries as well as tourists (the Czech foreign ministry is just up the road, and Margaret Thatcher once dined here). In summer get a table in its leafy *zahradní restaurace* (garden restaurant) across the street. (☏220 941 244; www.restaurantuzlatehrusky.cz; Nový Svět 3; mains 450-700Kč; ⏰11am-1am; 🚊22)

Malý Buddha ASIAN €

7 Map p34, A3

Candlelight, incense and a Buddhist shrine characterise this intimate, vaulted restaurant that tries to capture the atmosphere of an oriental tearoom. The menu is a mix of Asian influences, with authentic Thai, Chinese and Vietnamese dishes, many of them vegetarian, and a drinks list that includes ginseng wine, Chinese rose liqueur and all kinds of tea.

Credit cards are not accepted. (☏220 513 894; www.malybuddha.cz; Úvoz 46; mains 140-250Kč; ⏰noon-10.30pm Tue-Sun; 🍴; 🚊22)

Host MEDITERRANEAN, ASIAN €€

8 Map p34, B3

Hidden away down a narrow staircase between streets, Host impresses with its sleekly modern dining room, decorated with old monochrome photos, and the stunning view from its outdoor terrace. Friendly staff will guide you through a competent menu that ranges from steaks, burgers and traditional Czech dishes to Asian favourites such as spring rolls and Thai-style prawn stir-fry. (☏728 695 793; www.hostrestaurant.cz; Loretánská 15; mains 300-400Kč; 🛜; 🚊22)

Understand
Curse of the Czech Crown Jewels

In St Vitus Cathedral, on the southern side of the Chapel of St Wenceslas, there's a small door locked with seven keys. In a nod to the biblical 'seven seals' of Revelations, each is in the safekeeping of a separate official.

What lies beyond this secretive and carefully guarded door? The Czech crown jewels, of course. They're rarely exhibited to the public, but the oldest among them is the 22-carat-gold St Wenceslas Crown, made for Charles IV in 1347 and dedicated to the earlier prince.

Like all the best regal artefacts, the crown comes with a legendary curse: any usurper wearing it is doomed to die within the year. Call it coincidence, but the Nazi chief of Prague, Reinhard Heydrich, donned the crown in 1941 and was duly assassinated in 1942 by the Czechoslovak resistance.

Drinking

Pivnice U Černého Vola
PUB

 9 Map p34, B3

Many religious people make a pilgrimage to the Loreta, but just across the road, the 'Black Ox' is a shrine that pulls in pilgrims of a different kind. This surprisingly inexpensive beer hall is visited by real-ale aficionados for its authentic atmosphere and lip-smackingly delicious draught beer, Velkopopovický Kozel (30Kč for 0.5L), brewed in a small town southeast of Prague. (☑220 513 481; Loretánské náměstí 1; ☉10am-10pm; 🚊22)

U Zavěšeného Kafe
BAR

 10 Map p34, C3

A superb drinking den barely five minutes' walk from the castle. Head for the back room, quirkily decorated with weird art and mechanical curiosities by local artist Kuba Krejci, and an ancient jukebox. Foaming Pilsner Urquell is 38Kč a half-litre, and the coffee is damn fine too. (☑605 294 595; www.uzavesenyhokafe.cz; Úvoz 6; ☉11am-midnight; 🛜; 🚊12, 20, 22)

Klášterní pivovar Strahov
BREWERY

11 Map p34, A4

Dominated by two polished copper brewing kettles, this convivial little pub serves up two varieties of its St Norbert beer: *tmavý* (dark), a rich, tarry brew with a creamy head, and *polotmavý* (amber), a full-bodied, hoppy lager; both are 59Kč per 0.4L. There's also a strong (6.3% alcohol by volume) IPA-style beer. (Strahov Monastery Brewery; ☑233 353 155; www.klasterni-pivovar.cz; Strahovské nádvoří 301; ☉10am-10pm; 🚊22)

Antique violins on display

Shopping

Houpací Kůň   TOYS

12 🔒 Map p34, A3

The 'Rocking Horse' toyshop houses a
collection of wooden folk dolls, 1950s
wind-up tractors, toy cars and –
surprise – even a couple of rocking
horses. There are quality toys and art
supplies you won't find anywhere else
in Prague, but for a typically Czech
souvenir try the famous and ubiquitous 'Little Mole' cartoon character,
available here in several guises. (📞603
515 745; Loretánské náměstí 3; 🕑9.30am-
6.30pm; 🚃22, 25)

Antique Music Instruments   ANTIQUES

13 🔒 Map p34, A4

It may not get the prize for most inventive shop name, but this place is a
real treasure trove of vintage stringed
instruments. You'll find an interesting
stock of antique violins, violas and
cellos dating from the 18th century to
the mid-20th century, as well as bows,
cases and other musical accessories.
(📞220 514 287; Pohořelec 9; 🕑9am-6pm;
🚃22)

Explore

Malá Strana & Petřín Hill

Almost too picturesque for its own good, the baroque district of Malá Strana (Little Quarter) tumbles down the hillside between Prague Castle and the river. The focal point here is Malostranské náměstí, the main square, dominated by the green dome of St Nicholas Church. Petřín Hill, topped by a park and faux-but-fun Eiffel Tower, rises south of the square.

The Sights in a Day

☀ Start your day on Malostranské náměstí: grab a coffee at **Malostranská beseda** (p55) to fortify yourself and admire the baroque splendour of **St Nicholas Church** (p47). Stroll the area's beautiful lanes and then stop by the **Karel Zeman Museum** (p48), **Kampa Museum** (p48) or the **Museum of the Infant Jesus of Prague** (p48) for some film, art or religious art. Grab lunch at **Cukrkávalimonáda** (p52).

☀ After lunch, you've got an uphill choice. If you've got kids in tow, hike or (better yet) take the **Funicular** (p43) to Petřín Hill and its host of kid-friendly activities, including an impressive **Lookout Tower** (p43) and **Mirror Maze** (p43). Another option is to climb **Nerudova** (p49) starting from behind Malostranské náměstí, noting the characteristic medieval signs on the doors of the houses.

☾ For the evening, dine riverside on the terrace of **Hergetova Cihelna** (p50) or go for something slightly higher-quality at **Elegantes** (p50). Afterwards, take in some for jazz at **U Malého Glena** (p54) or catch a local band at **Malostranská beseda** (p55). For drinks, there's **Mlýnská Kavárna** (p52) or the ever-crazy **Blue Light** (p54).

For a local's day in the Gardens of Malá Strana, see p44.

 Top Sights

Petřín Hill (p42)

 Local Life

Gardens of Malá Strana (p44)

♥ **Best of Prague**

Bars & Pubs
Blue Light (p54)

Mlýnská Kavárna (p52)

Food
Elegantes (p50)

Café Savoy (p50)

Hergetova Cihelna (p50)

Museums
Franz Kafka Museum (p49)

Karel Zeman Museum (p48)

Museum of the Infant Jesus of Prague (p48)

Culture
U Malého Glena (p54)

Malostranská beseda (p55)

Getting There

🚊 **Tram** Take tram 12, 20 or 22 to Malostranské náměstí; or line 6, 9, 12, 20 or 22 to Újezd.

Ⓜ **Metro** The closest stop is Malostranská on Line A.

Top Sights
Petřín Hill

This 318m-high hill is one of Prague's largest green spaces. It's great for quiet, tree-shaded walks and fine views over the 'city of a hundred spires' from the observation deck of a highly convincing Eiffel Tower wannabe. There were once vineyards here, and a quarry that provided the stone for most of Prague's Romanesque and Gothic buildings. Take the funicular railway up to add a bit of a day-trip feel.

Map p46, B3

admission to park free

lookout tower 10am-10pm Apr-Sep, to 8pm Mar & Oct, to 6pm Nov-Feb

6, 9, 12, 20, 22 to Újezd

Autumn vista across Petřín Hill

Don't Miss

Petřín Funicular
First opened in 1891, the **Petřín Funicular Railway** (adult/child 32/16Kč; ⊙9am-11.30pm Apr-Oct, to 11.20pm Nov-Mar) trundles along 510m of track every 10 minutes (every 15 minutes from November to March) from Újezd to the Petřín Lookout Tower, with a stop at Nebozízek.

Petřín Lookout Tower
Some of the best views of Prague – including, on a clear day, the Central Bohemian forests – are from the top of this 62m-tall **tower** (adult/child 120/65Kč), built in 1891 for the Prague Exposition. The Eiffel Tower lookalike has 299 steps (and a lift).

Memorial to the Victims of Communism
The striking Memorial to the Victims of Communism sculpture shows disintegrating human figures descending a staggered slope. A bronze plaque records the terrible human toll of the communist era: 205,486 arrested; 170,938 driven into exile; 248 executed; 4500 who died in prison; and 327 shot trying to escape.

Mirror Maze
The **Mirror Maze** (adult/child 75/55Kč; ⊙10am-10pm Apr-Sep, 10am-8pm Mar & Oct, 10am-6pm Nov-Feb), just below the Lookout Tower, was also built for the 1891 Prague Exposition. The maze of distorting mirrors was based on the Prater in Vienna; there's also, inexplicably, a diorama of the 1648 Battle of Prague.

☑ Top Tips

▶ Before heading up the hill, stop at a bakery or supermarket to pick up picnic fixings. There are lots of benches and places to spread a blanket.

▶ Hiking up Petřín Hill is a pleasant alternative to the funicular and not too strenuous if you follow the winding paths.

▶ Ride the funicular at night for glittering views out over the city.

▶ Instead of taking the funicular down, consider walking northward through the top of the park towards Strahov Monastery.

✗ Take a Break

Restaurant Nebozízek (p50) is located halfway up Petřín Hill's funicular route – it offers wonderful views and is also accessible by foot.

Café Savoy (p50), not far from the funicular base station, is great for either coffee or lunch.

Local Life
Gardens of Malá Strana

The aristocrats who inhabited Malá Strana in the 17th and 18th centuries sculpted beautiful baroque gardens, many of which are open to the public. From April to October, whenever the sun shines the neighbourhood's parks and gardens fill up with local students toting sketchbooks, young mothers with kids, and business types relaxing on their lunch breaks. Note that from November to March many of the parks are closed.

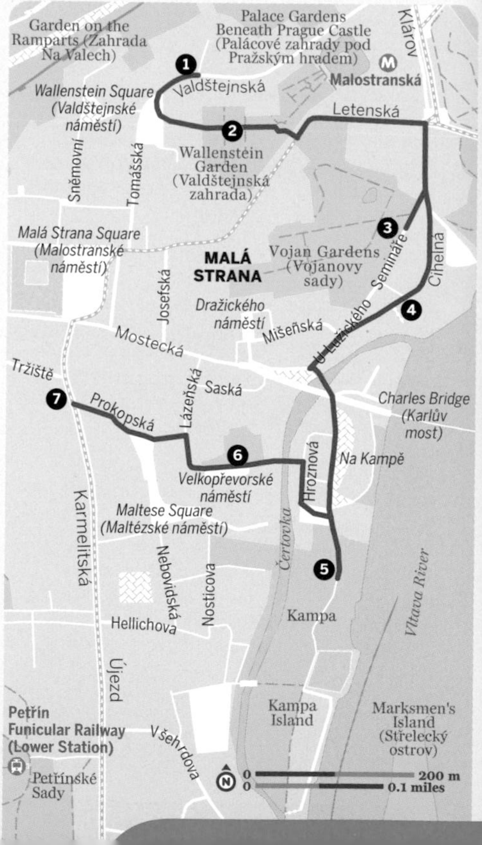

❶ Stroll the Gardens Beneath Prague Castle

The beautiful, terraced **Gardens Beneath Prague Castle** (adult/child 80/50Kč; ⏲10am-9pm Jun & Jul, to 8pm Aug, to 7pm May & Sep, to 6pm Apr & Oct), on the steep southern slopes below the castle, date from the 17th and 18th centuries. They were restored in the 1990s and contain a Renaissance loggia with frescos of Pompeii and a baroque portal with sundial that cleverly catches the sunlight reflected off a fountain's water.

2 Admire Wallenstein Garden

Baroque **Wallenstein Garden** (admission free; ⊙7.30am-7pm Mon-Fri, 10am-7pm Sat & Sun Jun-Sep, to 6pm daily Mar-Oct) is an oasis of peace amid the bustle of Malá Strana. Created for Duke Albrecht of Wallenstein in the 17th century, its finest feature is the huge loggia decorated with scenes from the Trojan Wars, flanked to one side by an enormous fake stalactite grotto dotted with carved grotesque faces.

3 Hang Out with Locals in Vojan Gardens

While less manicured than most of Malá Strana's parks, **Vojan Gardens** (⊙8am-dusk) is a popular spot with locals who like to come here to take a breather with the kids, sit in the sun or even hold summer parties.

4 Spot an Unusual Fountain

In the open-air plaza in front of the Franz Kafka Museum is a much-photographed public artwork: David Černý's sculpture **Proudy**. The quirky animatronic sculpture features two men relieving themselves into a puddle shaped like the Czech Republic. The microchip-controlled sculptures write out famous literary quotations of Prague with the streams.

5 Feel the Breeze at Kampa

Toss a frisbee, take a load off or just watch the local hipsters play with their dogs at the leafy riverside park known simply as Kampa (from the Latin campus or 'field'). One of the city's favourite chill-out zones, it's usually littered with lounging bodies – and excessively romantic teenagers – in summer.

6 Find Inner Peace

The **John Lennon Peace Wall** is a memorial graffiti wall to the former Beatle. After his murder in New York in 1980, Lennon became a pacifist hero for young Czechs; his image was painted on this wall opposite the French Embassy, along with political graffiti and Beatles lyrics.

7 Discover the Vrtbov Garden

The 'secret' **Vrtbov Garden** (adult/concession 62/52Kč; ⊙10am-6pm Apr-Oct), hidden along an alley at the corner of Tržiště and Karmelitská, was built in 1720 for the Earl of Vrtba, the senior chancellor of Prague Castle. It's a formal baroque garden, climbing steeply up the hillside to a terrace graced with baroque statues of Roman mythological figures by Matthias Braun.

E

Mánes Bridge (Mánesův most)

Franz Kafka Museum 6

Charles Bridge (Karlův most)

Vltava River

Klárov

Letenská

U Lužického semináře

28 9

Kampa Museum

Vojan Gardens (Vojanovy sady) 22

27 26

Karel Zeman Museum 2

Na Kampě

U Sovových mlýnů 3

Kampa Island

Čertovka

For reviews see

⊙ Top Sights	p42
⊙ Sights	p47
⊗ Eating	p50
⊗ Drinking	p52
⊕ Shopping	p55

Legion Bridge (Legii Most)

D

Wallenstein Garden (Valdštejnská zahrada)

Tomášská

MALÁ STRANA

10

Prague City Tourism

Míšeňská

Josefská

Saská

Lázeňská

Maltese Square 4

Velkopřevorské náměstí

14

Nebovidská

Hellichova

U Sovových mlýnů 19

Všehrdova 13

Říční

Vitězná 11

20

Újezd

Mostecká

Prokopská

Harantova

25 23

17 15

16

Karmelitská

C

Prague Castle (Pražský hrad)

Garden on the Ramparts (Zahrada Na Valech)

Thunovská

Sněmovní

Malá Strana Square (Malostranské náměstí)

St Nicholas Church 1

Tržiště

29 24

Museum of the Infant Jesus of Prague 5

18

Petřín Funicular Railway (Lower Station)

U Lanové Dráhy

Petřínské Sady

HRADČANY

Hradčany Square (Hradčanské náměstí)

Ke Hradu

Nerudova

Nerudova 7

Vlašská

21

Jánský vršek

Quo Vadis (David Černý Sculpture) 8

Vrtbov Garden (Vrtbovská zahrada)

Schönborská zahrada

Lobkovická zahrada

Seminářská zahrada

Nebozízek Station 12

Petřín Hill

Růžový sady

Petřín Funicular Railway (Upper Station)

U Kasáren

Úvoz

Loretánská

Kláštová

A

B

1

2

3

4

N

0 200 m

0 0.1 miles

St Nicholas Church, Mala Straná Square

Sights

St Nicholas Church

CHURCH

 Map p46, C2

Malá Strana is dominated by the huge green cupola of St Nicholas Church, one of Central Europe's finest baroque buildings. (Don't confuse it with the other Church of St Nicholas on Old Town Square.) On the ceiling, Johann Kracker's 1770 *Apotheosis of St Nicholas* is Europe's largest fresco (clever trompe l'œil technique has made the painting merge almost seamlessly with the architecture). (Kostel sv Mikuláše; ☎ 257 534 215; www.stnicholas.cz; Malostranské náměstí 38; adult/child 70/50Kč; ⊙9am-5pm Mar-Oct, to 4pm Nov-Feb; 🚊12, 20, 22)

St Nicholas Church Bell Tower

TOWER

During the communist era, the bell tower of St Nicholas Church (see 1 ⊙ Map p46, C2) was used to spy on the nearby American embassy – on the way up you can still see a small, white cast-iron urinal that was installed for the use of the watchers. Today it provides visitors with a grand view over Malá Strana and Charles Bridge. (http://en.muzeumprahy.cz/prague-towers; Malostranské náměstí; adult/child 90/65Kč; ⊙10am-10pm Apr-Sep, to 8pm Mar & Oct, to 6pm Nov-Feb; 🚊12, 20, 22)

Karel Zeman Museum   MUSEUM

2 ⦿ Map p46, D2

Bohemia-born director Karel Zeman (1910–69) was a pioneer of movie special effects, whose work is little-known outside the Czech Republic. This fascinating museum, established by his daughter, reveals the many tricks and techniques he perfected, and even allows visitors a bit of hands-on interaction – you can film yourself on your smartphone against painted backgrounds and 3D models. (Museum of Film Special Effects; ☏ 724 341 091; www. muzeumkarlazemana.cz; Saský dvůr, Saská 3; adult/child 200/140Kč; ◷10am-7pm, last admission 6pm; 🚃 12, 20, 22)

Kampa Museum   GALLERY

3 ⦿ Map p46, D3

Housed in a renovated mill building, this gallery is devoted to 20th-century

> **Local Life**
> ## Kampa Island
>
> A lovely little green oasis, Kampa Island is separated from Malá Strana proper by a canal known as the Devil's Stream (Čertovka). Two mill wheels survive, where washer-women used to do laundry until the 1930s. Nowadays, the peaceful island attracts mainly young families, dog-walkers and artists. Night-time views of the lights twinkling across the river are superb, particularly from the south of the island. Take tram 6, 9, 12, 20, or 22 to Újezd.

and contemporary art from Central Europe. The highlights of the permanent exhibition are extensive collections of bronzes by Cubist sculptor Otto Gutfreund and paintings by František Kupka, a pioneer of abstract art. (Muzeum Kampa; ☏ 257 286 147; www. museumkampa.cz; U Sovových mlýnů 2; adult/concession 220/110Kč; ◷10am-6pm; 🚃 12, 20, 22)

Maltese Square   SQUARE

4 ⦿ Map p46, D2

References to the Knights of Malta around Malá Strana hark back to 1169, when that military order established a monastery in the Church of Our Lady Beneath the Chain on this square. Disbanded by the communists, the Knights have regained much property under post-1989 restitution laws, including the Lennon Wall. (Maltézské náměstí; 🚃 12, 20, 22)

Museum of the Infant Jesus of Prague   MUSEUM

5 ⦿ Map p46, C3

The **Church of Our Lady Victorious** (kostel Panny Marie Vítězné), built in 1613, has on its central altar a 47cm-tall waxwork figure of the baby Jesus, brought from Spain in 1628 and known as the **Infant Jesus of Prague** (Pražské Jezulátko). At the back of the church is a museum displaying a selection of the frocks used to dress the Infant. (Muzeum Pražského Jezulátka; ☏ 257 533 646; www.pragjesu.info; Karmelitská 9; admission free; ◷church 8.30am-7pm

Understand
The Numbers Game

Until numbering was introduced in the 18th century, exotic house names and signs were the only way of identifying individual Prague buildings. This practice came to a halt in 1770, when it was banned by the city councillors.

More such-named houses and signs survive on **Nerudova** than along any other Prague street. As you head downhill look out for At the Two Suns (No 47), the Golden Horseshoe (No 34), the Three Fiddles (No 12), the Red Eagle (No 6) and the Devil (No 4). Other signs include a St Wenceslas on horseback (No 34), a golden key (No 27) and a golden goblet (No 16).

Mon-Sat, to 8pm Sun, museum 9.30am-5.30pm Mon-Sat, 1-6pm Sun, closed 1 Jan, 25 & 26 Dec & Easter Mon; 🚊12, 20, 22)

Franz Kafka Museum
MUSEUM

6 ◎ Map p46, E2

This much-hyped exhibition on the life and work of Prague's most famous literary son, entitled 'City of K', explores the intimate relationship between the writer and the city that shaped him, through the use of original letters, photographs, quotations, period newspapers and publications, and video and sound installations. (Muzeum Franzy Kafky; ☎257 535 373; www.kafkamuseum.cz; Cihelná 2b; adult/child 200/120Kč; ◷10am-6pm; 🚊12, 20, 22, Ⓜ Malostranská)

Nerudova
STREET

7 ◎ Map p46, B1

Following the tourist crowds downhill from the castle via Ke Hradu, you will arrive at Nerudova, architecturally the most important street in Malá Strana; most of its old Renaissance facades were 'baroquefied' in the 18th century. It's named after the Czech poet Jan Neruda (famous for his short stories, *Tales of Malá Strana*), who lived at the **House of the Two Suns** (dům U dvou slunců; Nerudova 47) from 1845 to 1857. (🚊12, 20, 22)

Quo Vadis (David Černý Sculpture)
MONUMENT

8 ◎ Map p46, B2

This golden Trabant car on four legs is a David Černý tribute to 4000 East Germans who occupied the garden of the then–West German embassy in 1989, before being granted political asylum and leaving their Trabants behind. You can see the sculpture through the fence behind the German embassy. Head uphill along Vlašská, turn left into a children's park, and left again to find it. (Where Are You Going; Vlašská 19; 🚊12, 20, 22)

Eating

Hergetova Cihelna

MEDITERRANEAN, ASIAN €€€

9 Map p46, E2

Housed in a converted 18th-century *cihelná* (brickworks), this place enjoys one of Prague's hottest locations, with a riverside terrace offering sweeping views of Charles Bridge and the Old Town waterfront. The menu is as sweeping as the view, ranging from seafood and upmarket burgers to Asian dishes such as Thai beef salad and chicken stir-fry. You'll also find there's a decent kids' menu and play area. (296 826 103; www.kampagroup.com; Cihelná 2b; mains 300-600Kč; 11.30am-1am; ; M Malostranská)

Elegantes

CZECH, EUROPEAN €€€

10 Map p46, D1

Hidden away in the historic Augustine Hotel (check out the ceiling fresco in the bar), this sophisticated yet relaxed restaurant is well worth seeking out. The menu ranges from down-to-earth, but delicious, dishes such as veal shank braised in the hotel's own St Thomas beer, to inventive dishes built around Czech game, such as wild boar ragout with chestnut pappardelle. (266 112 280; www.elegantes.cz; Letenská 12; mains 490-990Kč; noon-10.30pm; ; 12, 20, 22)

Café Savoy

EUROPEAN €€

11 Map p46, D4

The Savoy is a beautifully restored belle époque cafe, with haughty black-and-white-suited waitstaff and a Viennese-style menu of hearty soups, salads, roast meats and schnitzels. There's also a good breakfast menu with plenty of healthy choices, including a 'Full English', an American breakfast, and eggs cooked half a dozen ways. (257 311 562; http://cafesavoy.ambi.cz; Vítězná 5; mains 125-500Kč; 8am-10.30pm Mon-Fri, 9am-10.30pm Sat & Sun; ; 6, 9, 12, 20, 22)

Restaurant Nebozízek

INTERNATIONAL €€

12 Map p46, B4

This 17th-century conservatory restaurant halfway up Petřín Hill now has a designer interior, with lots of pale Nordic furniture and Singapore orchids, as well as a menu that peppers its modern international menu with a few Czech staples. The views are fabulous, even if the place feels touristy. (257 315 329; www.nebozizek.cz; Petřínské sady 411; mains 150-420Kč; 11am-10pm; 6, 9, 12, 20, 22 to Újezd, then Petřín funicular)

Bar Bar

CZECH, EUROPEAN €€

13 Map p46, D4

This friendly cellar bar is frequented more by locals than tourists, but the healthy-eating menu is chalked on a blackboard in both Czech and English. It ranges from chicken breast with

Outdoor dining, Malá Strana Square

honey, lemon and chilli to grilled salmon with creamed spinach, with a couple of good veggie alternatives. The weekday lunch menu offers soup and a main course for 120Kč. (☎257 312 246; www.bar-bar.cz; Všehrdova 17; mains 170-320Kč; ☺noon-midnight Mon-Sat, to 6pm Sun; ✐; ⬚6, 9, 12, 20, 22)

U Malé Velryby
SEAFOOD, MEDITERRANEAN €€

14 ✗ Map p46, D3

'The Little Whale' is a tiny place – only eight tables – run by chef-proprietor Jason (from Cork, Ireland), who gets fresh seafood flown in daily from French markets. The seafood chowder is tasty and filling, the braised pork

ribs with cauliflower and sesame puree are tender, and the tapas exceedingly moreish. Make sure Jason himself is in the kitchen for a top-quality dinner. (☎257 214 703; www. umalevelryby.cz; Maltézské náměstí 15; mains 360-410Kč; ☺10am-10pm; ⬚12, 20, 22)

Café de Paris
FRENCH €€

15 ✗ Map p46, D2

A little corner of France tucked away on a quiet square, the Café de Paris is straightforward and unpretentious. So is the menu – onion soup or foie gras terrine to start, followed by entrecôte steak with chips, salad and a choice of sauces (they're very proud of the Café de Paris sauce, made to a 75-year-old recipe). Daily specials include a vegetarian alternative. (☑603 160 718; www.cafedeparis.cz; Maltézské náměstí 4; mains 245-425Kč; ⊙noon-midnight; ⬚12, 20, 22)

Cukrkávalimonáda EUROPEAN €

16 Map p46, D2

A cute little cafe-cum-restaurant that combines minimalist modern styling with Renaissance-era painted timber roof-beams, CKL offers fresh, homemade pastas, frittatas, ciabattas, salads and pancakes (sweet and savoury) by day and a slightly more sophisticated bistro menu in the early evening. There's also a good breakfast menu offering ham and eggs, croissants, and yoghurt – and the hot chocolate is to die for. (☑257 225 396; www.cukrkavalimonada.com; Lázeňská 7; mains 100-200Kč; ⊙9am-7pm; ⬚12, 20, 22)

U Modré Kachničky CZECH €€€

17 Map p46, D3

A plush and chintzy 1930s-style hunting lodge hidden away on a quiet side street, 'At the Blue Duckling' is a pleasantly old-fashioned place with quiet, candlelit nooks perfect for a romantic dinner. The menu is heavy on traditional Bohemian duck and game dishes, such as roast duck with *slivovice* (plum brandy), plum sauce and potato pancakes. (☑257 320 308; www.umodrekachnicky.cz; Nebovidská 6; mains 450-600Kč; ⊙noon-4pm & 6.30pm-midnight; 🛜; ⬚12, 20, 22)

Noi THAI €€

18 Map p46, C4

A restaurant that feels a bit like a club, Noi is superstylish but with a chilled-out, oriental atmosphere. The decor is based around lotus blossoms, lanterns and soft lighting, and the menu follows the Asian theme with competent Thai dishes such as chicken in red curry, and pad thai noodles, which – unusually for a Prague restaurant – have a hefty chilli kick. (☑257 311 411; www.noirestaurant.cz; Újezd 19; mains 180-290Kč; ⊙11am-1am; 🛜; ⬚12, 20, 22)

Drinking

Mlýnská Kavárna BAR

19 Map p46, D4

This cafe-bar in Kampa Park has existed in various guises since the communist era, and you might still hear it called Tato Kejkej, its previous incarnation, or just Mlýn (the mill). A wooden footbridge leads from Kampa to the smoky, dimly lit interior, which is peopled with local artists (David Černý is a regular), writers and politicians (look out for Czech statesman Karel Schwarzenberg). (☑257 313 222; Všehrdova 14; ⊙noon-midnight; 🛜; ⬚6, 9, 12, 20, 22)

Sampling Czech beers, Malá Strana

Klub Újezd
BAR

20 Map p46, D4

Klub Újezd is one of Prague's many 'alternative' bars, spread over three floors (DJs in the cellar, and a cafe upstairs) and filled with a fascinating collection of original art and weird wrought-iron sculptures. Clamber onto a two-tonne bar stool in the agreeably grungy street-level bar, and sip on a beer beneath a scaly, fire-breathing sea monster. (251 510 873; www.klubujezd.cz; Újezd 18; 2pm-4am; 6, 9, 12, 20, 22)

Baráčnická Rychta
BEER HALL

21 Map p46, C2

Tucked away along a winding street, this atmospheric 19th-century beer hall feels a bit furtive and secretive. In the small upstairs bar you can sup four types of Svijanský beer as well as the more common Pilsner Urquell; food is also served. Downstairs, the larger Cabaret Hall hosts big bands and offbeat live gigs. (257 532 461; www.baracnickarychta.cz; Tržiště 23; 11am-11pm Mon-Sat, to 9pm Sun; 12, 20, 22 to Malostranské náměstí)

Understand
Kafka's Neighbourhood
- -

'Someone must have been telling lies about Josef K, for without having done anything wrong, he was arrested one fine morning' – that opening line to Franz Kafka's *The Trial* (1925) is widely considered among the greatest in world literature. The words are also a testament to Prague's disorientating nature; and in the writer's home city it's hard not to be moved by his genius. Of course, it's simple to pay tribute to Kafka by visiting his birthplace or grave, but true fans will want to use the opportunity to delve more into the novelist's complex relationship with Prague, which he complained was small and claustrophobic but got under your skin. The Franz Kafka Museum (p49) is just the place.

Kafíčko
CAFE

22 🚇 Map p46, D2

This little cafe, with cream walls, bentwood chairs, fresh flowers and arty photographs, is an unexpected setting for some of Prague's best tea and coffee. Choose from a wide range of quality roasted beans from all over the world, freshly ground and made into espresso, cappuccino or latte (40Kč to 55Kč). (☎724 151 795; Míšeňská 10; ⏰10am-10pm; 👶; 🚊12, 20, 22)

Blue Light
COCKTAIL BAR

23 🚇 Map p46, D2

The Blue Light is a dark and atmospheric hang-out, as popular with locals as with tourists, where you can sip a caipirinha or cranberry colada as you cast an eye over the vintage jazz posters, records, old photographs and decades-worth of scratched graffiti that adorn the walls. The background jazz is recorded rather than live, and never overpowers your conversation. Often heaving on weekend nights. (☎257 533 126; www.bluelightbar.cz; Josefská 1; ⏰6pm-3am; 🚊12, 20, 22)

U Malého Glena
BAR, JAZZ

24 🚇 Map p46, C2

'Little Glen's' is a lively, American-owned bar and restaurant where hard-swinging local jazz or blues bands play every night in the cramped and steamy stone-vaulted cellar. There are Sunday-night jam sessions where amateurs are welcome (as long as you're good). It's a small venue, so get here early if you want to see as well as hear the band. (☎257 531 717; www.malyglen.cz; Karmelitská 23; ⏰10am-2am, to 3am Fri & Sat, music from 8.30pm; 📶; 🚊12, 20, 22)

Malostranská beseda
BAR, CLUB

25 Map p46, D1

Malá Strana's four-storey pleasure palace reopened in 2010 after a five-year reconstruction. The fabled music club on the 2nd floor is better than ever, with a lively roster of cabaret acts, jazz and old Czech rockers. There's also an art gallery on the top floor and a big beer hall in the basement, with a bar and restaurant on the ground floor. (257 409 123; www.malostranska-beseda.cz; Malostranské náměstí 21; shows 120-250Kč; bar 4pm-1am, box office 5-9pm Mon-Sat, to 8pm Sun; 12, 20, 22)

Shopping

Marionety Truhlář
ARTS & CRAFTS

26 Map p46, D2

On a back street beneath the western end of Charles Bridge, this palace of puppetry stocks traditional marionettes from more than 40 workshops around the Czech Republic, as well as offering DIY puppet kits, courses on puppet-making, and the chance to order a custom-made marionette in your own (or anyone else's) likeness. (606 924 392; www.marionety.com; U Lužického semináře 5; 10am-7pm; 12, 20, 22)

Artěl
GLASS, INTERIOR DESIGN

27 Map p46, D2

Traditional Bohemian glassmaking meets modern design in this stylish shop founded by US designer Karen Feldman. In addition to hand-blown designer crystal, you can find a range of vintage and modern items of Czech design, from jewellery and ceramics to toys and stationery. (www.artelglass.com; U Lužického semináře 7; 10am-7pm; 12, 20, 22)

Shakespeare & Sons
BOOKS

28 Map p46, D2

Though its shelves groan with a formidable range of literature in English, French and German, this is more than just a bookshop – it's a congenial literary hang-out with knowledgable staff, occasional author events, and a cool downstairs space for sitting and reading. Also has Prague's best range of titles on Eastern European history. (257 531 894; www.shakes.cz; U Lužického semináře 10; 11am-9pm; 12, 20, 22)

Pavla & Olga
FASHION

29 Map p46, C2

Sisters Pavla and Olga Michalková originally worked in the film and TV industry before setting up their own fashion label, creating a unique collection of quirky and cute hats, clothes and accessories. Past customers have included Czech supermodel Tereza Maxová, Britpop band Blur and photographer Helmut Newton. (728 939 872; Tržiště 3; 2-6pm Mon-Fri; 12, 20, 22)

Local Life
Beer & Culture in Smíchov

Standing in contrast to the fairy-tale historic sphere of castles and royal gardens, working-class Smíchov is a mainly industrial district on the Vltava's western bank. With its vibrant contemporary-art scene and unpretentious bars, the slightly gritty neighbourhood offers an authentic taste of Czech life, though its character is slowly changing with the construction of modern office complexes and an influx of new businesses.

Getting There

Ⓜ Line B to Anděl.

🚌 Lines 4, 7, 9, 10, 12, 14, 16 and 20 all pass through Smíchov, stopping at Anděl.

❶ Jazz on the River

Jazz Dock (www.jazzdock.cz; cover 150Kč; ⏱4pm-3am), Smíchov's riverside jazz venue, is a step up from the typical Prague club, with clean, modern decor and a romantic view out over the Vltava. It draws some of the best international acts. Go early or book to get a good table.

❷ Avant-Garde Theatre at Švandovo divadlo

The funky **Švandovo divadlo** (www. svandovodivadlo.cz; tickets 150-300Kč; ⏱box office 2-8pm Mon-Fri, 2hr before performances Sat & Sun) stages avant-garde dramatic pieces, many with English subtitles, and acoustic music performances. It also hosts art exhibits and events.

❸ Modern Art at Futura

The **Futura Gallery** (www.futuraprojekt. cz; admission by donation; ⏱11am-6pm Wed-Sun) is home to *Brown-nosers* (2003) by David Černý: stick your head inside the statue's backside to see a video of the former Czech president and the National Gallery's director feeding each other baby food.

❹ Czech Food at Zlatý klas

Cosy Pilsner Urquell restaurant **Zlatý klas** (www.zlatyklas.cz; mains 130-200Kč; ⏱11am-11pm Sun-Thu, 11.30am-1am Fri & Sat) is beloved for its hearty, well-prepared Czech cuisine – try the killer 'Charles IV' baked pork ribs – plus ultrafresh *tankova* (tanked) beer.

❺ Dancing at the 'Bulldog'

Popular pub **Hospoda U Buldoka** (www. ubuldoka.cz; ⏱bar 11am-midnight Mon-Thu, 11am-1am Fri, noon-midnight Sat, noon-11pm Sun, club 8pm-4am Mon-Sat) is a great place to drink – and a surprisingly good place to let your hair down too. Don't expect sophisticated club ambience: this is a beer-fuelled, dance-till-you-drop joint.

❻ Beer at the Staropramen Brewery

To soak up some of Smíchov's down-to-earth charm – and feel the gentrification that's currently underway – pull up a barstool at **Na Verandách** (www.phnaverandach.cz; mains 150-280Kč; ⏱11am-midnight Mon-Wed, to 1am Thu-Sat, to 11pm Sun), housed in the Staropramen Brewery (operating since 1871). In summer sit outside on the terrace.

❼ Cultural Events at 'Meet Factory'

For cutting-edge film screenings, concerts, theatrical performances and art installations, find out what's happening at David Černý's **Meet Factory** (www.meetfactory.cz; admission free), a multifaceted gallery and entertainment venue (look for hanging red cars on the outside).

Explore

Jewish Museum & Josefov

Peaceful Josefov is the site of the former Jewish ghetto – the physical, cultural and spiritual home to the city's Jewish population for nearly 800 years. While many Jews left the quarter when it was renovated in the early 20th century (and tens of thousands were killed in the Holocaust), the surviving synagogues and cemetery make up the popular Jewish Museum.

The Sights in a Day

☼ Arrive at the **Jewish Museum** (p60) first thing in the morning and head for the **Old Jewish Cemetery** (p62) – the place is much more atmospheric when you're not with a huge crowd. Stop in at the **Maisel Synagogue** (p61) and the **Pinkas Synagogue** (p61), then take a well-deserved coffee break at **Bakeshop Praha** (p65) – and treat yourself to a chocolate croissant while you're at it. Properly caffeinated? Move on to a minitour of the beautiful **Spanish Synagogue** (p61).

☼ Stop for a late lunch – including a beer, of course – at classy corner pub **Kolkovna** (p66). You'll be near the **Franz Kafka Monument** (p65), which is fun for a quick look (and photo op). Spend the rest of the afternoon at either the **Museum of Decorative Arts** (p65) for design or the **Convent of St Agnes** (p65) for medieval and Gothic art.

☾ For dinner, there's **Lokál** (p66) for a classic Czech meal or **Chagall's** (p66) for something French and fancier. Afterwards, choose from a classical concert at the **Dvořák Hall** (p70) or opt for an edgier evening at the hollowed-out former theatre **Roxy** (p70). Before or after the show, stop in at **Tretter's New York Bar** (p67) for an expertly prepared martini.

👁 Top Sights

Jewish Museum (p60)

Old Jewish Cemetery (p62)

🖤 Best of Prague

Bars & Pubs

Kolkovna (p66)

Tretter's New York Bar (p67)

U Rudolfina (p67)

Food

Bakeshop Praha (p65)

Lokál (p66)

Chagall's (p66)

History

Old-New Synagogue (p65)

Spanish Synagogue (p61)

Shopping

Boheme (p71)

TEG (p70)

Dušní 3 (p71)

Getting There

Ⓜ **Metro** Line A to Staroměstská.

🚊 **Tram** Lines 17, 18 to Staroměstská; lines 5, 8, 26 to Dlouhá třída.

Top Sights
Jewish Museum

Prague's Jewish Museum is among the city's most visited sights. It was established in 1906 to preserve artefacts from the quarter after it was razed and renovated in the late-19th and early-20th centuries. Exhibits are scattered among a handful of synagogues and focus on Jewish life and traditions. Highlights include the Pinkas Synagogue and its memorial to Czech and Moravian Jews killed in the Holocaust.

◉ Map p64, B3

www.jewishmuseum.cz

adult/child 300/200Kč, combined ticket incl entry to Old-New Synagogue 480/320Kč

⊘9am-6pm Sun-Fri Apr-Oct, to 4.30pm Nov-Mar

Ⓜ Staroměstská

Holocaust memorial, Pinkas Synagogue

Don't Miss

Klaus Synagogue & Ceremonial Hall

Both the baroque **Klaus Synagogue** (Klauzová synagóga; U starého hřbitova 1) and the nearby Ceremonial Hall (Obřadní síň) contain exhibits on Jewish health and burial traditions and will be of most interest to historians or devout visitors.

Maisel Synagogue

Mordechai Maisel was mayor of the Jewish quarter under the liberal rule of Emperor Rudolf II during the 16th century. He was also the richest man in the city of Prague; in addition to various public works, he paid for this **synagogue** (Maiselova synagóga; Maiselova 10) to be built for his private use. Today, it houses rotating exhibitions.

Pinkas Synagogue

Built in 1535, this **synagogue** (Pinkasova synagóga; Široká 3) was used for worship until 1941; it's now a moving Holocaust memorial, its walls inscribed with the names, birth dates and dates of disappearance of 77,297 Czech Jews. Also here is a poignant exhibition of drawings made by children held at the Terezín concentration camp (north of Prague) during World War II.

Spanish Synagogue

Considered the most beautiful of the museum's synagogues, this 19th-century Moorish-style **building** (Španělská synagóga; Vězeňská 1) boasts an ornate interior, an exhibition on recent Jewish history and a handy bookshop.

☑ Top Tips

▶ The museum is closed on Saturdays and Jewish holidays.

▶ Entry is by combined ticket only; it's not possible to visit the sites individually.

▶ Men must cover their heads. Yarmulkes (skullcaps) are provided at entrances.

▶ The Old-New Synagogue is not considered part of the museum and requires a separate admission ticket.

✗ Take a Break

Stop for some of the city's best gourmet coffee and pastries at nearby Bakeshop Praha (p65).

For a good pint of beer in the vicinity of the Spanish Synagogue, head to corner pub Kolkovna (p66).

Top Sights
Old Jewish Cemetery

City authorities once insisted that deceased Jews be interred only here – nowhere else – so by the time this cemetery stopped taking new burials in 1787 it was full to bursting. Today it holds more than 12,000 tombstones – though as the Jewish Museum points out, many more than that are buried here. Be aware that conditions at this popular attraction sometimes feel almost as crowded for the living as for the dead.

Map p64, A3

www.jewishmuseum.cz

Pinkas Synagogue, Široká 3

included in admission to Jewish Museum

9am-6pm Apr-Oct, to 4.30pm Nov-Mar

Staroměstská

Old Jewish Cemetery

Don't Miss

Rabbi Loew's Tomb

Sometimes called 'the Jewish hero of the Czechs', Rabbi Judah Loew ben Bezalel (1525–1609) was a respected scholar and the chief rabbi of Bohemia in the 16th century. Perhaps more importantly to Czech people, he's part of a legend surrounding the creation of the Golem (p66), a creature he supposedly built from clay to protect the Jewish people living in Prague's ghetto.

Mordechai Maisel's Tomb

This tomb honours a philanthropist with some incredibly deep pockets. In addition to serving as a Jewish leader in the 16th century, Maisel was the city's wealthiest citizen. He paid for the construction of new buildings in the ghetto, had the roads paved, commissioned the Maisel Synagogue (p61) for his own private use and even lent money to Emperor Rudolf II.

David Gans' Tomb

A noted German historian and astronomer, Gans came to Prague in part to hear the lectures of Rabbi Loew. He's perhaps most famous for his association with Tycho Brahe, who asked Gans to translate the Alphonsine Tables from Hebrew to German.

Joseph Solomon Delmedigo's Tomb

Another impressive Jewish intellectual represented in the cemetery is Joseph Solomon Delmedigo, who was both a physician and a philosopher. He studied and worked all over Europe before finally settling in Prague in 1648 to write various scientific texts.

JAMES STRACHAN/GETTY IMAGES ©

☑ Top Tips

▶ Entry to the cemetery is included in the general Jewish Museum admission ticket.

▶ Arrive early as the cemetery gets increasingly busy as the day goes on.

▶ Remember that you're in a cemetery – always be careful where you step.

✗ Take a Break

Stylish Mistral Cafe (p67) is a short walk from the cemetery and is great for coffee or food.

Also nearby is U Rudolfina (p67), a down-to-earth local pub with some of the city's best Pilsner Urquell.

For reviews see

◎	Top Sights	p60
◉	Sights	p65
✕	Eating	p65
🍷	Drinking	p67
🎭	Entertainment	p70
🛍	Shopping	p70

200 m
0.1 miles

Kotva

Benediktská

Rybná

Rybná

Jakubská

Haštalská

Malá Štupartská

16

7

Dlouhá

Masná

Masná

Rámová

10

21

Tyn
Courtyard
(Týnský dvůr)

Týnská uličk

U obecního dvora

13

Haštalské
náměstí

3

Convent of
St Agnes

Kozí

Týnská ulička

Kozí

8

12

5

Týnská uličk

JOSEFOV

Bílkova

Veleslavína

6 18

V Kolkovně

11

20

19

Dlouhá

Old Town Square
(Staroměstské náměstí)

Dvořákovo nábřeží

U Milosrdných

Dušní

Dušní

Salvátorská

Franz Kafka
Monument

4

17

PRAHA 1

Pařížská

Jáchymova

Eliška Krásnohorské

Intercontinental
Hotel

Old-New
Synagogue

1

Červená

Prague Jewish
Museum

Maiselova

Kaprova

Žatecka

Široká

Museum of
Decorative Arts

2

Old Jewish
Cemetery

Staroměstská

9

Valentinská

Vltava River

Čech Bridge
(Čechův most)

Dvořákovo nábřeží

17.listopadu

15

Jan Palach Square
(náměstí Jana
Palacha)

Křižovnická

Sights

Old-New Synagogue
SYNAGOGUE

 1 Map p64, B3

Completed around 1270, the Old-New Synagogue is Europe's oldest working synagogue and one of Prague's earliest Gothic buildings. You step down into it, as it predates the raising of Staré Město's street level in medieval times to guard against floods. Men must cover their heads (a hat or bandanna will do; paper yarmulkes are handed out at the entrance). (Staronová synagóga; www.jewishmuseum.cz; Červená 2; adult/child 200/140Kč; ⊙9am-6pm Sun-Fri Apr-Oct, to 4.30pm Nov-Mar; 🚊17)

Museum of Decorative Arts
MUSEUM

 2 Map p64, A3

This museum opened in 1900 as part of a European movement to encourage a return to the aesthetic values sacrificed to the Industrial Revolution. Its four halls are a feast for the eyes, full of 16th- to 19th-century artefacts such as furniture, tapestries, porcelain and a fabulous collection of glasswork. (Umělecko-průmyslové muzeum; 251 093 111; www.upm.cz; 17.listopadu 2; whole gallery adult/child 120/70Kč, temp exhibition only 80/40Kč; ⊙10am-7pm Tue, to 6pm Wed-Sun; 🚊17)

Convent of St Agnes
GALLERY

3 Map p64, D2

In the northeastern corner of Staré Město is the former Convent of St Agnes, Prague's oldest surviving Gothic building. The 1st-floor rooms hold the National Gallery's permanent collection of medieval and early-Renaissance art (1200–1550) from Bohemia and Central Europe, a treasure house of glowing Gothic altar paintings and polychrome religious sculptures. (Klášter sv Anežky; 224 810 628; www.ngprague.cz; U Milosrdných 17; adult/child 150/80Kč; ⊙10am-6pm Tue-Sun; 🚊5, 8, 24)

Franz Kafka Monument
MONUMENT

4 Map p64, C3

Commissioned by Prague's Franz Kafka Society in 2003, Jaroslav Róna's unusual sculpture of a mini Kafka riding on the shoulders of a giant empty suit was based on the writer's story *Description of a Struggle,* in which the author explores a fantasy landscape from the shoulders of 'an acquaintance' (who may be another aspect of the author's personality). (cnr Vězeňská & Dušní; Ⓜ Staroměstská)

Eating

Bakeshop Praha
BAKERY, SANDWICHES €

 5 Map p64, D3

This fantastic bakery sells some of the best bread in the city, along with pastries, cakes, sandwiches, wraps, salads and quiche. Very busy at lunchtime. (222 316 823; www.bakeshop.cz; Kozí 1; sandwiches 75-200Kč; ⊙7am-9pm; Ⓜ Staroměstská)

Understand
Golem City

Tales of golems, or servants created from clay, date back to early Judaism. However, the most famous such mythical creature belonged to 16th-century Prague's Rabbi Loew, of the Old-New Synagogue. Loew is said to have used mud from the Vltava's banks to create a golem to protect the Prague ghetto. However, left alone one Sabbath, the creature ran amok and Rabbi Loew was forced to rush out of a service and remove the magic talisman that kept it moving. He then carried the lifeless body into the synagogue's attic, where some insist it remains. In 1915, Gustav Meyrink's novel *Der Golem* reprised the story and brought it into the European mainstream.

Kolkovna
CZECH €€

 6 Map p64, C3

Owned and operated by the Pilsner Urquell brewery, Kolkovna is a stylish, modern take on the traditional Prague pub, with decor by top Czech designers, and posh (but hearty) versions of classic Czech dishes such as goulash, roast duck and Moravian sparrow (a cut of roast pork with a side of bread and dumplings), as well as the Czech favourite, roast pork knuckle. All washed down with exquisite Urquell beer, of course. (☏224 819 701; www.kolkovna-restaurant.cz; V Kolkovně 8; mains 110-360Kč; ☺11am-midnight; ☎; Ⓜ Staroměstská)

Lokál
CZECH €

 7 Map p64, E3

Who'd have thought it possible? A classic Czech beer hall (albeit with slick modern styling); excellent *tankové pivo* (tanked Pilsner Urquell); a daily changing menu of traditional Bohemian dishes; efficient, friendly service; and a no-smoking area! Top restaurant chain Ambiente has turned its hand to Czech cuisine, and the result has been so successful that the place is always busy, mostly with locals. (☏222 316 265; http://lokal-dlouha.ambi.cz; Dlouhá 33; mains 110-270Kč; ☺11am-1am Mon-Fri, noon-1am Sat, noon-10pm Sun; ☐5, 8, 24)

Chagall's
FRENCH €€€

 8 Map p64, D3

Stylishly understated decor in black, white and grey (with a hint of a Czech cubist vibe) is leavened with splashes of colour from old oil paintings and coloured fabrics in this sophisticated dining room. But it's the warmth of the welcome you notice first, closely followed by the quality of the menu – fresh seasonal produce prepared with Gallic care and flair. (☏739 002 347; www.chagalls.cz; Kozí 5; mains lunch 160-300Kč, dinner 460-510Kč; ☺11am-midnight; ☎; ☐5, 8, 24)

Mistral Café
BISTRO €

9 Map p64, A4

Is this the coolest bistro in the Old Town? Pale stone, bleached birchwood and potted shrubs make for a clean, crisp, modern look, and the clientele of local students and office workers clearly appreciate the competitively priced, well-prepared food. Fish and chips in crumpled brown paper with lemon and black-pepper mayo – yum! (✆222 317 737; www.mistralcafe.cz; Valentinská 11; mains 100-260Kč; ⏰10am-11pm; 🛜; MStaroměstská)

Fish & Chips
FISH & CHIPS €€

10 Map p64, D3

Prague's first proper fish-and-chip shop goes a bit over the top with its 'British' theme, sporting white London Underground tiles, chandeliers, a red telephone box, and photos of the Beatles, Prince Charles and a Mini. But the eponymous signature dish is pretty good – crisp battered cod and chunky chips, with malt vinegar and Heinz ketchup. Takeaway available. (✆606 881 414; http://fishandchipsprague. cz; Dlouhá 21; mains 200-270Kč; ⏰11am-midnight Sun-Thu, to 1am Fri & Sat; 🚊5, 8, 24)

Drinking

Tretter's New York Bar
BAR

11 Map p64, C3

This sultry 1930s Manhattan-style cocktail bar harks back to gentler times when people went out for night-caps – and when the drinks were stiff and properly made. Regularly cited as one of the city's top bars, Tretter's brings in the beautiful people and has prices to match. Book your table in advance. (✆224 811 165; www.tretters.cz; V Kolkovně 3; ⏰7pm-2am; MStaroměstská)

Kozička
BAR

12 Map p64, D3

The 'Little Goat' is a buzzing, red-brick basement bar decorated with cute goat sculptures, serving Krušovice on tap at 45Kč for 0.5L, though watch out: the bartenders will occasionally sling you a *tuplák* (a German-style 1L

Local Life

Beer from a Tank

To counter growing interest among Czech beer-drinkers in microbrews and regional beers, the big national brewers have come up with some gimmicks of their own. The most popular of these is *tankové pivo* ('tank' beer), where beer is delivered and stored in enormous tanks (instead of smaller kegs) to keep it fresher and more flavourful.

Several nearby pubs offer tank beer, including the ever-popular pubs Lokál and Kolkovna, as well as old-school joints like **U Rudolfina** (✆222 328 758; Křižovnická 10; ⏰11am-10pm; MStaroměstská). Look for the sign *'pivo z tanku'* (beer from the tank).

Understand
Jewish Prague

Jews have been part of Prague for as long as it has existed, though their status has ebbed and flowed. For centuries, Jews were restricted to living in a small corner of the Old Town (today's Josefov). Some periods brought terror and pogroms, while others – the early 17th century – brought prosperity. In the 19th century, Jews were allowed to live outside their ghetto, but a century later most were murdered by the occupying Nazis.

Early Oppression
Jews began living in Prague in the 10th century, and by the 11th century the city was one of Europe's most important Jewish centres. The Crusades marked the start of the Jews' plight as the city's oldest synagogue was burned to the ground. By the end of the 12th century, they lost many rights; soon they were forced into a walled ghetto that was locked at night. For years, Jews remained third-class citizens while emperors and the nobility argued over who should be in charge of Jewish affairs.

The Golden Age
The mid-16th to early 17th century is considered the golden age of Jewish history. Emperor Rudolf II (r 1576–1612) worked closely with Mayor Mordechai Maisel (1528–1601), at the time the wealthiest man in Prague. The community was led in spirit by noted mystic and Talmudic scholar Rabbi Loew (1525–1609).

Emancipation came in the 18th century under Habsburg Emperor Josef II. In 1848, Jews won the right of abode, meaning they could live where they wanted. The ghetto's walls were torn down and the Jewish quarter was renamed Josefov (to honour Josef II). As wealthy Jews moved out, the area slid into squalor. At the end of the 19th century, the area was levelled and rebuilt in art nouveau splendour.

Destruction & Preservation
The Jewish community was largely destroyed by the Nazis in World War II, and only a few thousand Jews remain. One historic irony is that many of the Jewish Museum's holdings come from *shtetls* (Jewish villages) liquidated by the Nazis. Hitler had the artefacts brought here, chillingly, to build a 'museum of an extinct race'.

Czech draught beer

mug) if they think you're a tourist. It fills up later in the evening with a mostly Czech crowd, and makes a civilised setting for a late-night session. (☏224 818 308; www.kozicka.cz; Kozí 1; ⊙4pm-4am Mon-Thu, 5pm-4am Fri, 6pm-4am Sat, 7pm-3am Sun; 🛜; Ⓜ Staroměstská)

James Joyce   PUB

13 🍺 Map p64, D2

You probably don't go to Prague to visit an Irish bar, but if you're here in winter this friendly pub offers something rarely seen in Prague bars: an open fire. Toast your toes while sipping a Guinness, or downing the all-day Irish breakfast fry, including Clonakilty black pudding. (☏224 818 851; www.jamesjoyceprague.cz; U obecního dvora 4; ⊙11am-12.30am Sun-Thu, to 2am Fri & Sat; 🛜; 🚋5,8,24)

Prague Beer Museum   PUB

14 🍺 Map p64, E3

Although the name seems aimed at the tourist market, this lively and always heaving pub is very popular with Praguers. There are no fewer than 30 Czech-produced beers on tap (plus a beer menu with tasting notes to guide you). Try a sample board – a wooden platter with five 0.15L glasses containing five beers of your choice. (☏732 330 912; www.praguebeer museum.com; Dlouhá 46; ⊙noon-3am; 🛜; 🚋5, 8, 24)

Entertainment

Dvořák Hall
CONCERT VENUE

15 ⭐ Map p64, A3

The Dvořák Hall in the neo-Renaissance **Rudolfinum** (☏227 059 270; www.ceskafilharmonie.cz; Alšovo nábřeží 12; ☐17, 18) is home to the world-renowned Czech Philharmonic Orchestra (Česká filharmonie). Sit back and be impressed by some of the best classical musicians in Prague. (Dvořákova síň; ☏227 059 227; www.ceskafilharmonie.cz; náměstí Jana Palacha 1; tickets 120-800Kč; ⏱box office 10am-12.30pm & 1.30-6pm Mon-Fri; Ⓜ Staroměstská)

Roxy
CLUB, PERFORMING ARTS

16 ⭐ Map p64, E2

Set in the ramshackle shell of an art deco cinema, the legendary Roxy has nurtured the more independent and innovative end of Prague's club spectrum since 1987 – this is the place to see the Czech Republic's top DJs. On the 1st floor is NoD, an 'experimental space' that stages drama, dance, performance art, cinema and live music. Best nightspot in Staré Město. (☏224 826 296; www.roxy.cz; Dlouhá 33; cover Fri & Sat free-300Kč; ⏱7pm-5am; ☐5, 8, 24)

Image Theatre
PERFORMING ARTS

17 ⭐ Map p64, C4

Founded in 1989, this company uses creative black-light theatre along with pantomime, modern dance and video – not to mention liberal doses of slapstick – to tell its stories. The staging can be very effective, but the atmosphere is often dictated by audience reaction. (Divadlo Image; ☏222 314 448; www.imagetheatre.cz; Pařížská 4; tickets 480Kč; ⏱box office 9am-8pm; Ⓜ Staroměstská)

Shopping

TEG
FASHION

18 Map p64, C3

TEG (Timoure et Group) is the design team created by Alexandra Pavalová and Ivana Šafránková, two of Prague's most respected fashion designers. This boutique showcases their quarterly collections, which feature a sharp, imaginative look that adds zest and sophistication to everyday, wearable clothes. There's a second branch near Národní třída. (☏222 327 358; www.timoure.cz; V Kolkovně 6; ⏱10am-7pm Mon-Fri, 11am-5pm Sat; Ⓜ Staroměstská)

Klara Nademlýnská
FASHION

19 Map p64, C4

Klara Nademlýnská is one of the Czech Republic's top fashion designers, having trained in Prague and worked for almost a decade in Paris. Her clothes are characterised by clean lines, simple styling and quality materials, making for a very wearable range that covers the spectrum from swimwear to evening wear via jeans, halter tops, colourful blouses and sharply styled suits. (☏224 818 769;

www.klaranademlynska.cz; Dlouhá 3; ⏰10am-7pm Mon-Fri, to 6pm Sat; Ⓜ Staroměstská)

Bohème FASHION

20 🔒 Map p64, C3

This boutique showcases the designs of Hana Stocklassa and her associates, with collections of knitwear, leather and suede clothes for women. Sweaters, turtlenecks, suede skirts, linen blouses, knit dresses and stretch denim suits seem to be the stock in trade, and there's a range of jewellery to choose from as well. (☎ 224 813 840; www.boheme.cz; Dušní 8; ⏰11am-7pm Mon-Fri, to 5pm Sat; Ⓜ Staroměstská)

Granát Turnov JEWELLERY

21 🔒 Map p64, D3

Part of the country's biggest jewellery chain, Granát Turnov specialises in Bohemian garnet, and has a huge range of gold and silver rings, brooches, cuff links and necklaces featuring these small, blood red stones. There's also pearl and diamond jewellery,

Q Local Life
Home of Fashion Boutiques

Josefov is home to the nascent Czech fashion scene, particularly small, independent boutiques that highlight the best of local and international design. For the latter, check out **Dušní 3** (☎ 234 095 870; www.dusni3.cz; Dušní 3; ⏰10am-7pm Mon-Sat; Ⓜ Staroměstská), a self-styled alternative to the megabrand stores on nearby Pařížská. You'll find a range of ready-to-wear fashion and accessories from top designers, including Tara Jarmon, Ilaria Nistri and Vivienne Westwood. They've got an excellent line of shoes and sunglasses as well.

and less expensive pieces set with the dark-green semiprecious stone known in Czech as *vltavín* (moldavite). (☎ 222 315 612; www.granat.eu; Dlouhá 28-30; ⏰10am-6pm Mon-Fri, to 1pm Sat; Ⓜ Náměstí Republiky)

Explore

Old Town Square & Staré Město

Staré Město (Old Town), with its evocative medieval square, maze of alleyways, and quirky sights like the Astronomical Clock, is the beating heart of the historic centre. Its origins date back to the 10th century, when a marketplace emerged on the Vltava's eastern bank. A thousand years later, it's as alive as ever, and surprisingly little changed by time.

Vertical text along left edge: WWW.CREATIVEPHOTOGRAPHY.GR BY SPYROS TAVITAV/GETTY IMAGES ©

The Sights in a Day

For the quietest experience and most magical views of **Charles Bridge** (p76), start your morning as early as possible. Start on the Malá Strana side and cross the bridge towards the Old Town. Be sure to climb the **Old Town Bridge Tower** (p77). Then make a beeline for the **Astronomical Clock** (p75) to catch the famous hourly chiming before the tourist crowds start to multiply.

Afterwards, take the lift up the **Old Town Hall Tower** (p75) for views over Old Town Square and the historic centre. Have a leisurely lunch at **Kalina** (p81), sampling gourmet versions of Czech dishes from the tasting menu. Then, wander the quaint cobblestone backstreets around Betlémské náměstí, stopping in to see Jan Hus' old stomping ground at **Bethlehem Chapel** (p80).

As night falls, head back to Old Town Square to view the beautifully illuminated **Church of St Nicholas** (p75) and **Church of Our Lady Before Týn** (p75). Have dinner on the terrace of **U Prince** (p81) or take a glass of Moravian wine in a glamorous setting at the Municipal House's cafe (p84). Catch some live jazz at **AghaRTA Jazz Centrum** (p86) to finish off the day.

 Top Sights

Old Town Square & Astronomical Clock (p74)

Charles Bridge (p76)

Best of Prague

Bars & Pubs
Hemingway Bar (p84)
Čili Bar (p84)
U Tří růží (p83)

Food
V Zátiší (p82)
Kalina (p81)
George Prime Steak (p83)

Museums
Charles Bridge Museum (p77)
Kinský Palace (p80)

Getting There

M **Metro** Take line A to Staroměstská (the closest stop to Old Town Square) or line A or B to Můstek.

Tram Lines 17 and 18 run to Staroměstská; lines 5, 8 and 26 stop at Dlouhá třída.

Top Sights
Old Town Square & Astronomical Clock

Laid with cobblestones and surrounded by spectacular baroque churches, soaring spires, candy-coloured buildings and a rococo palace, Old Town Square is an architectural smorgasbord and a photographer's delight. While the Astronomical Clock – a mechanical marvel that still chimes on the hour – is more than 600 years old, many of Old Town Square's structures are even older: settlers started moving here across the river from Prague Castle as far back as the 10th century.

◉ Map p78, C2

Staroměstské náměstí

Ⓜ Staroměstská

Astronomical Clock, Old Town Square

Don't Miss

Astronomical Clock

Built in 1490 by a master clockmaker named Hanuš, the Astronomical Clock was a scientific feat in its day – even after various renovations, it remains a paradigm of antique technology. On the hour (from 9am to 9pm), crowds gather below for its quaint visual display (p80).

Old Town Hall Clock Tower

Old Town Hall, dating from 1338, has more to offer than its clock. Climb (or take the lift) up the **clock tower** (Věž radnice; Staroměstské náměstí 1; adult/child 100/50Kč, incl Old Town Hall 160Kč; ⏲11am-10pm Mon, 9am-10pm Tue-Sun) for privileged views over Old Town Square and the historic city centre.

Jan Hus Statue

Sitting near the centre of the square, Ladislav Šaloun's brooding art nouveau statue of Jan Hus was unveiled on 6 July 1915, the 500th anniversary of Hus' death at the stake.

Church of Our Lady Before Týn

Straight out of a 15th-century fairy tale, the spiky, spooky Gothic spires of **Church of Our Lady Before Týn** (Kostel Panny Marie před Týnem; suggested donation 25Kč; ⏲10am-1pm & 3-5pm Tue-Sat, 10.30am-noon Sun Mar-Oct, shorter hours Nov-Feb), aka Týn Church, are an unmistakable Old Town landmark. It also houses the tomb of Tycho Brahe.

Church of St Nicholas

This pretty baroque **monastery** (Kostel sv Mikuláše; admission free; ⏲10am-4pm) is relatively new: finished in 1735, it replaced a Gothic church built here in the late 13th century. After several incarnations it now serves as a Czechoslovak Hussite church and a classical concert venue.

☑ Top Tips

▶ For the best views of the Astronomical Clock, come to the chiming at 9am or 10am. Arrive a few minutes before the hour.

▶ Look for lively food and craft stalls in Old Town Square around major holidays like Christmas and Easter.

▶ Climb (or take the lift) up the clock tower for spectacular views over Old Town Square. Again, earlier is better.

▶ The most romantic time to visit the square is after dark, when the medieval buildings are beautifully illuminated.

✕ Take a Break

Have a gourmet lunch at Kalina (p81), where fresh Czech produce is given a serious gastronomic twist.

At night, you're spoiled for choice. Čili Bar (p84) is a perfect romantic hideway. Hemingway Bar (p84) has the city's best cocktails, but reserve in advance.

Top Sights
Charles Bridge

You know a historic landmark is something special when even the crush of tourist traffic hardly takes away from its magnificence. So it is with Charles Bridge, Prague's signature monument. Commissioned in 1357, the massive, 520m-long stone bridge was the only link across the Vltava River between Prague Castle and the Old Town until 1741. It's particularly awe-inspiring at dawn, when the silhouettes of saintly statues along both sides seem to guide you towards the towering hilltop fortress.

 Map p78, A2

Karlův most

admission free

⊘24hr

🚊17, 18 to Karlovy lázně, 12, 20, 22 to Malostranské náměstí

Charles Bridge at dawn

Don't Miss

View from the Old Town Bridge Tower

Perched at the eastern end of Charles Bridge, the elegant late-14th-century **Old Town Bridge Tower** (Staroměstská mostecká věž; adult/child 90/65Kč; ☺10am-10pm Apr-Sep, to 8pm Mar & Oct, to 6pm Nov-Feb) was built not only as a fortification but also as a triumphal arch marking the entrance to the Old Town. Head upstairs for the dramatic view down over the crowded bridge.

Saintly Statues

The first monument erected on the bridge was the crucifix near the eastern end, in 1657. The first statue – the Jesuits' 1683 tribute to St John of Nepomuk – inspired other Catholic orders, and over the next 30 years a score more went up. Today most are copies, but a few of the originals can be seen at the Brick Gate & Casements (p111) at the Vyšehrad Citadel.

Rubbing St John of Nepomuk

The most famous statue is that of St John of Nepomuk, on the northern side of the bridge about halfway across. According to legend, Wenceslas IV had him thrown off the bridge in 1393 for refusing to divulge the queen's confessions (he was her priest). Tradition says if you rub the bronze plaque, you will one day return to Prague.

Charles Bridge Museum

Examine the history of the Vltava's most famous crossing at the **Charles Bridge Museum** (Muzeum Karlova Mostu; Křížovnické náměstí 3; adult/concession 150/70Kč; ☺10am-8pm May-Sep, to 6pm Oct-Apr), located near the bridge's Old Town entrance. When you learn about the bridge's tumultuous 650-year history, including at least two perilous encounters with floods, you'll be surprised it's still standing.

ILAN SHACHAM/GETTY IMAGES ©

☑ Top Tips

▶ Visit the bridge early in the day to beat the crowds.

▶ Keep your valuables close at hand: pickpockets lurk here, especially in summer.

▶ Plan to cross the bridge at least twice – once towards the castle and once away from it.

▶ Sunrise is the ideal time for photos. In winter if it starts snowing, head for the bridge to capture some unforgettable images.

✕ Take a Break

Not far from the entrance to the Old Town side of the bridge, the student cafe Krásný ztráty (p84) is a great place to relax over a coffee or beer.

Splurge on a gourmet meal paired with Czech wine at Bellevue (p82) or V zátiší (p82); both are close to the Old Town side of the bridge.

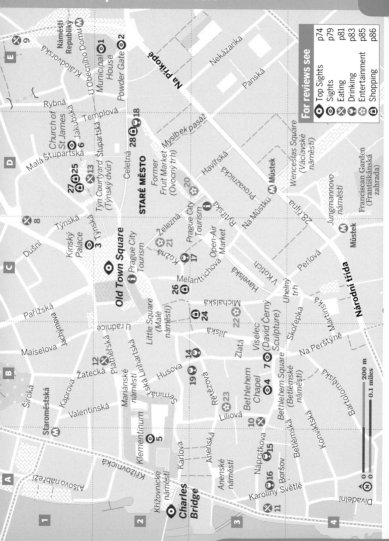

For reviews see

◎	Top Sights	p74
◎	Sights	p79
⊗	Eating	p81
⊗	Drinking	p83
⊕	Entertainment	p85
⊕	Shopping	p86

Náměstí Republiky Ⓜ

Králodvorská

⊗ 9

U Obecního Domu Ⓜ

Municipal ◎1
House

Powder Gate ◎2

Na Příkopě

Nekázanka

Panská

Rybná

Templová

Church of
St James ◎6

Jakubská

Štupartská

Celetná

28 Ⓜ 18

Mysibek pasáž

Former
Fruit Market
(Ovocný trh)

◎20

Havířská

Malá Štupartská

27 Ⓜ 25

⊗ 13

Týn Courtyard
(Týnský dvůr)

STARÉ MĚSTO

Provaznická

Na Můstku Ⓜ Můstek

Wenceslas Square
(Václavské
náměstí)

Jungmannovo
náměstí

Franciscan Garden
(Františkánská
zahrada)

Ⓜ Můstek

Týnská ◎3

Kinský
Palace

⊗ 8

Dušní

Prague City
Tourism ◎

Old Town Square ◎

ⓘ Prague City
Tourism

Železná

Kožná

◎21

Prague City
Tourism ◎

Rytířská

Perlová

28. října

Melantrichova

Havelská

V kotcích

Uhelný
trh

Pařížská

Úřadnice

Little Square
(Malé
náměstí)

◎26

◎24

Michalská

⊕ 22

Viselec
(David Černý
Sculpture) ◎7

Skořepská

Na Perštýně

Národní třída

Maiselova

12 ⊕

Platnéřská

Mariánské
náměstí

Jilská

Zlatá

Bethlehem Square
(Betlémské
náměstí)

Konviktská

Bartolomějská

Široká

Kaprova

Žatecká

Linhartská

Seminář

Husova

◎19 14

Řetězová

Bethlehem
Chapel ◎4

⊗ 23

Liliová

Anenská

Náprstkova

Betlémská

Staroměstská Ⓜ

Valentinská

Klementinum ◎5

Karlova

Anenské
náměstí

10 ⊗

15 ⊕

16 ⊕

U Borša

Karoliny Světlé

⊗ 11

Divadelní

Alšovo nábřeží

Křižovnická

Křižovnické
náměstí

Charles
Bridge ◎

200 m
0.1 miles

JOHN FREEMAN/GETTY IMAGES ©

Municipal House and Powder Gate

Sights

Municipal House   HISTORIC BUILDING

1 👁 Map p78, E2

Restored in the 1990s after decades of neglect, Prague's most exuberant and sensual building is a labour of love, every detail of its design and decoration carefully considered, every painting and sculpture loaded with symbolism. The restaurant and cafe flanking the entrance are like walk-in museums of art nouveau design; upstairs are half a dozen sumptuously decorated halls that you can visit by guided tour. (Obecní dům; 📞 222 002 101; www.obecnidum.cz; náměstí Republiky 5; guided tour adult/child under 10/concession 290/free/240Kč; ⊙ public areas 7.30am-11pm, information centre 10am-8pm; Ⓜ Náměstí Republiky)

Powder Gate   TOWER

2 👁 Map p78, E2

The 65m-tall Powder Gate was begun in 1475 on the site of one of Staré Město's original 13 gates. The tower above the arch houses exhibitions of medieval weapons and instruments, many of which were used in films shot in Prague (including *Van Helsing, Chronicles of Narnia* and *Blade II*), but the main attraction is the view from the top. (Prašná brána; http://en.muzeumprahy.cz/prague-towers; Na příkopě; adult/child 90/65Kč; ⊙ 10am-10pm Apr-Sep, to 8pm Oct & Mar, to 6pm Nov-Feb; Ⓜ Náměstí Republiky)

Kinský Palace

GALLERY

3 Map p78, C1

The late-baroque Kinský Palace sports Prague's finest rococo facade, completed in 1765 by the redoubtable Kilian Dientzenhofer. Today, the palace is home to a branch of the National Gallery, housing its collection of ancient and oriental art, ranging from ancient Egyptian tomb treasures and Greek Apulian pottery (4th century BC) to Chinese and Japanese decorative art and calligraphy. (Palác Kinských; 📞224 810 758; www.ngprague.cz; Staroměstské náměstí 12; adult/child 150/80Kč; 🕙10am-6pm Tue-Sun; Ⓜ Staroměstská)

Bethlehem Chapel

CHURCH

4 Map p78, B3

The Bethlehem Chapel is a national cultural monument, being the birthplace of the Hussite cause. Jan Hus preached here from 1402 to 1412, marking the emergence of the Reform movement from the sanctuary of the Karolinum (where he was rector). Every year on the night of 5 July, the eve of Hus' burning at the stake in 1415, a memorial is held here with speeches and bell-ringing. (Betlémská kaple; 📞224 248 595; Betlémské náměstí 3; adult/child 60/30Kč; 🕙10am-6.30pm Apr-Oct, to 5.30pm Nov-Mar; 🚋6, 9, 18, 21, 22)

Understand

The Astronomical Clock's Spectacle

Every hour on the hour, crowds gather beneath the Old Town Hall Tower to watch the Astronomical Clock in action. It's an amusing – if slightly underwhelming – performance – that takes just under a minute to finish. Most people simply stand and gawk, but it's worth understanding a bit of the clock's historic (and highly photogenic) symbolism.

The four figures beside the clock represent the deepest civic anxieties of 15th-century Praguers: **Vanity** (with a mirror), **Greed** (with his telltale money bag), **Death** (the skeleton) and **Pagan Invasion** (represented by a Turk). The four figures below these are the Chronicler, Angel, Astronomer and Philosopher.

On the hour, Death rings a bell and inverts his hourglass, and the Twelve Apostles parade past the windows above the clock, nodding to the crowd. On the left side are Paul (with a sword and a book), Thomas (lance), Jude (book), Simon (saw), Bartholomew (book) and Barnabas (parchment); on the right side are Peter (with a key), Matthew (axe), John (snake), Andrew (cross), Philip (cross) and James (mallet). At the end, a cock crows and the hour is rung.

Klementinum
HISTORIC BUILDING

 5 Map p78, A2

The Klementinum is a vast complex of beautiful baroque and rococo halls, now mostly occupied by the Czech National Library. Most of the buildings are closed to the public, but you can walk freely through the courtyards, or take a 50-minute guided tour of the baroque Library Hall, the Astronomical Tower and the Chapel of Mirrors. (📞222 220 879; www.klementinum.cz; entrances on Křížovnická, Karlova & Mariánské náměstí; guided tour adult/child 220/140Kč; ⏰10am-5pm Apr-Oct, to 4pm Nov, Dec & Mar; Ⓜ Staroměstská)

Church of St James
CHURCH

 6 Map p78, D1

The great Gothic mass of the Church of St James began in the 14th century as a Minorite monastery church, and was given a beautiful baroque facelift in the early 18th century. But in the midst of the gilt and stucco is a grisly memento: on the inside of the western wall (look up to the right as you enter) hangs a shrivelled human arm. (Kostel sv Jakuba; Malá Štupartská 6; admission free; ⏰9.30am-noon & 2-4pm Tue-Sat, 2-4pm Sun; Ⓜ Náměstí Republiky)

Viselec (David Černý Sculpture)
ART

 7 Map p78, B3

Here's more inspired madness from artist David Černý. Look up as you walk along Husova street; you'll see a

bearded, bespectacled chap – looking not unlike Sigmund Freud – casually dangling by one hand from a pole way above the street. (Hanging Out; Husova; 🚊6, 9, 18, 21, 22)

Eating

Kalina
FRENCH €€€

 8 Map p78, C1

Setting a trend for taking the best of fresh Czech produce and giving it the French gourmet treatment, this smart but unfailingly friendly little restaurant offers dishes such as duck pâté with rowan berries, smoked eel with beetroot and hazelnut, and roast wild boar with red wine and juniper. The set two-course lunch menu costs 330Kč. (📞222 317 715; www.kalinarestaurant.cz; Dlouhá 12; mains 330-720Kč; ⏰noon-3pm & 6-11.30pm Mon-Sat; 📶; 🚊5, 8, 24)

Ambiente Pizza Nuova
ITALIAN €€

9   Map p78, E1

This cool 1st-floor space, filled with big tables and banquettes with picture windows overlooking náměstí Republiky, showcases a good idea from the Ambiente team: for a fixed price (298Kč per person before 6pm, 365Kč after) you get an all-you-can-eat pasta and pizza deal. (Without the deal, the salad and antipasti buffet and pizza-pasta combined costs 475/555Kč.) Wine by the glass is 75Kč to 120Kč. (☎221 803 308; pizzanuova.ambi.cz; Revoluční 1; mains 165-500Kč; ☺11.30am-11.30pm; ☎ 🚻; Ⓜ Náměstí Republiky)

V zátiší
INTERNATIONAL, MODERN CZECH €€€

10 Map p78, B3

'Still Life' is one of Prague's top restaurants, famed for the quality of its cuisine. The decor is bold and modern, with quirky glassware, boldly patterned wallpapers and cappuccino-coloured crushed-velvet chairs. The menu ranges from high-end Indian cuisine to gourmet versions of traditional Czech dishes – the South Bohemian duck with cabbage and herb dumplings is superb. (☎222 221 155; www.vzatisi.cz; Liliová 1; 2-/3-course meal 990/1090Kč; ☺noon-3pm & 5.30-11pm; ☎; 🚋17, 18)

Bellevue
INTERNATIONAL €€€

11 Map p78, A3

Book a table on the terrace and come to enjoy the fabulous views of the river and castle while tucking into gourmet cuisine. Bellevue offers a Eurasian choice of dishes, from roasted veal loin in black-truffle crust to New Zealand lamb chops marinated in lemon thyme. Best value are two- and three-course set menus. (☎224 221 443; www.bellevuerestaurant.cz; Smetanovo nábř 18; set menu 2/3 courses 1190/1490Kč; ☺11am-11pm; 🚹; 🚋17, 18 to Karlovy lázně)

◯ Local Life
Going Meatless in Staré Město

Prague's oldest quarter is home to several good vegetarian and vegan spots. Our favourites:

Maitrea (☎221 711 631; www.restaurace-maitrea.cz; Týnská ulička 6; weekday lunch 115Kč; mains 145-165Kč; ☺11.30am-11.30pm Mon-Fri, noon-11.30pm Sat & Sun; 🚹; Ⓜ Staroměstská) Beautifully designed space with inventive vegetarian dishes.

Lehká Hlava (☎222 220 665; www.lehkahlava.cz; Boršov 2; mains 150-185Kč; ☺11.30am-11.30pm Mon-Fri, noon-11.30pm Sat & Sun; 🚹🚻; 🚋17, 18) Down a narrow cul-de-sac, this simple, student-friendly spot exists in a little world of its own.

Country Life (☎224 213 366; www.countrylife.cz; Melantrichova 15; mains 90-180Kč; ☺10.30am-7.30pm Mon-Thu, 10.30am-3.30pm Fri, noon-6pm Sun; ☎🚹; Ⓜ Můstek) All-vegan cafeteria offering inexpensive salads, vegetarian goulash, sunflower-seed burgers and soy drinks.

George Prime Steak

STEAKHOUSE €€€

12 Map p78, B2

The name of the game here is 100% Black Angus USDA (US Department of Agriculture) Prime Beef, imported from the American Midwest. Order a charcoal-broiled T-bone steak in the elegant surroundings of the main restaurant, or opt for a house burger in the less formal bar. The presence on the menu of the 1000Kč 'Oligarch Burger' (with foie gras and gold leaf) gives a clue as to the target market. (226 202 599; http://georgeprimesteak.com; Platnéřská 19; mains 350-1000Kč; noon-2.30pm & 6-10.30pm; ; Staroměstská)

Indian Jewel

INDIAN €€

13 Map p78, D1

A long, vaulted room in a medieval building makes an elegant setting for one of Prague's best Indian restaurants, with marble floors, chunky wooden chairs, copper tableware and restrained oriental decor; tables spill into the courtyard in summer. The food impresses too, with light and flaky parathas, richly spiced sauces and plenty of fire in the hotter curries. (222 310 156; www.indianjewel.cz; Týn 6; mains 300-400Kč; 11am-11pm; ; Staroměstská)

JOHN FREEMAN/GETTY IMAGES ©

Outdoor dining, náměstí Republiky

Drinking

U Tří růží

BREWERY

14 Map p78, B3

In the 19th century there were more than 20 breweries in Prague's Old Town, but by 1989 there was only one left (U Medvídku). The Three Roses brewpub, on the site of one of those early breweries, helps revive the tradition, offering six beers on tap, including a tasty *světlý ležák* (pale lager), good food and convivial surroundings. (601 588 281; www.u3r.cz; Husova 10; 11am-11pm Sun-Thu, to midnight Fri & Sat; 17, 18)

Kavárna Obecní dům

CAFE

The spectacular café in Prague's opulent Municipal House (see 1 Map p78, E2) offers the opportunity to sip your cappuccino amid an orgy of art nouveau splendour. Also worth a look is the neat little American Bar in the basement of the building, all polished wood, stained glass and gleaming copper. (☑222 002 763; www.kavarnaod.cz; náměstí Republiky 5; ☺7.30am-11pm; 🛜; Ⓜ Náměstí Republiky)

Krásný ztráty

CAFE

15 🍷 Map p78, A3

This cool cafe – the name translates to something like 'beautiful destruction' – doubles as an art gallery and occasional music venue, and is hugely popular with students from nearby Charles University. There are Czech newspapers and books to leaf through, chilled tunes on the sound system, and a menu of gourmet teas and coffees to choose from. (☑775 755 143; www.krasnyztraty.cz; Náprstkova 10; ☺9am-1am Mon-Fri, noon-1am Sat & Sun; 🛜; 🚊17, 18)

Hemingway Bar

COCKTAIL BAR

16 🍷 Map p78, A3

The Hemingway is a snug and sophisticated hideaway with dark leather benches, a library-like back room, flickering candlelight, and polite and professional bartenders. There's a huge range of quality spirits (especially rum), first-class cocktails, champagne and cigars. (☑773 974 764; www.hemingwaybar.eu; Karolíny Světlé 26; ☺5pm-1am Mon-Thu, 5pm-2am Fri, 7pm-2am Sat, 7pm-1am Sun; 🛜; 🚊17, 21)

Čili Bar

COCKTAIL BAR

17 🍷 Map p78, C2

This tiny cocktail bar could not be further removed in atmosphere from your typical Old Town drinking place. Cramped and smoky – there are Cuban cigars for sale – with battered leather armchairs competing for space with a handful of tables, it's friendly, relaxed and lively. Try the speciality of the house – rum mixed with finely chopped red chillis. (☑724 379 117; www.cilibar.cz; Kožná 8; ☺5pm-2am; 🛜; Ⓜ Můstek)

Grand Cafe Orient

CAFE

18 🍷 Map p78, D2

Prague's only cubist cafe, the Orient was designed by Josef Gočár in 1912 and flaunts its cubist styling down to the smallest detail, including the lampshades and coat hooks. It was restored and reopened in 2005, having been closed since 1920. Decent coffee and inexpensive cocktails, but occasionally surly service. (☑224 224 240; www.grandcafeorient.cz; Ovocný trh 19; ☺9am-10pm Mon-Fri, 10am-10pm Sat & Sun; Ⓜ Náměstí Republiky)

U Zlatého Tygra

PUB

19 🍷 Map p78, B3

The 'Golden Tiger' is one of the few Old Town drinking holes that has

Estates Theatre

hung on to its soul – and its reasonable prices (40Kč per 0.5L of Pilsner Urquell), considering its location. It was novelist Bohumil Hrabal's favourite place – there are photos of him on the walls – and where Václav Havel took Bill Clinton in 1994 to show him a real Czech pub. (☏222 221 111; www.uzlatehotygra.cz; Husova 17; ⌚3-11pm; Ⓜ Staroměstská)

Entertainment

Smetana Hall   CLASSICAL MUSIC

The Smetana Hall, centrepiece of the stunning Municipal House (see

1 ◎ Map p78, E2), is the city's largest concert hall, with seating for 1200. This is the home venue of the Prague Symphony Orchestra (Symfonický orchestr hlavního města Prahy), and it also stages performances of folk dance and music. (Smetanova síň; ☏222 002 101; www.obecnidum.cz; náměstí Republiky 5; tickets 300-600Kč; ⌚box office 10am-6pm; Ⓜ Náměstí Republiky)

Estates Theatre   OPERA, DANCE

20 ✪ Map p78, D3

The Estates is the oldest theatre in Prague, famed as the place where Mozart conducted the premiere of *Don Giovanni* on 29 October 1787.

Mozartissimo – a medley of highlights from several of Mozart's operas, including *Don Giovanni* – is performed here from March to May (see www.bmart. cz); the rest of the year sees various opera, ballet and drama productions. (Stavovské divadlo; ☑ 224 902 322; www. narodni-divadlo.cz; Ovocný trh 1; tickets 50-1290Kč; ⊙ box office 10am-6pm; Ⓜ Můstek)

AghaRTA Jazz Centrum
JAZZ

21 ⭐ Map p78, C2

AghaRTA has been staging top-notch modern jazz, blues, funk and fusion since 1991, but moved into this central Old Town venue only in 2004. A typical jazz cellar with red-brick vaults, the centre also has a music shop (open 7pm to midnight) that sells CDs, T-shirts and coffee mugs. As well as hosting local musicians, AghaRTA occasionally stages gigs by leading international artists. (☑ 222 211 275; www. agharta.cz; Železná 16; cover 250Kč; ⊙ 7pm-1am, music 9pm-midnight; Ⓜ Můstek)

Jazz Club U Staré Paní
JAZZ

22 ⭐ Map p78, C3

Located in the basement of the Hotel U Staré Paní, this long-established but recently revamped jazz club caters to all levels of musical appreciation. There's a varied program of modern jazz, soul, blues and Latin rhythms, and a dinner menu if you want to make a full evening of it. (☑ 605 285 211; www.jazzstarapani. cz; Michalská 9; cover 100-250Kč; ⊙ 7pm-1am Wed-Sun, music from 9pm; Ⓜ Můstek)

Blues Sklep
JAZZ

23 ⭐ Map p78, B3

One of the city's newer jazz clubs, the Blues Sklep (*sklep* means 'cellar') is a typical Old Town basement with dark, Gothic-vaulted rooms that provide an atmospheric setting for regular nightly jazz sessions. Bands play anything from trad New Orleans jazz to bebop, blues, funk and soul. (☑ 221 466 138; www.bluessklep.cz; Liliová 10; cover 100-150Kč; ⊙ bar 7pm-2.30am, music 9pm-midnight; 🚃 17, 18)

Shopping

Art Deco Galerie
ANTIQUES

24 🔒 Map p78, C3

Specialising in early-20th-century items, this shop has a wide range of 1920s and '30s stuff, including clothes, handbags, jewellery, glassware and ceramics, along with knick-knacks such as the kind of cigarette case you might imagine Dorothy Parker pulling from her purse. (☑ 224 223 076; www. artdecogalerie-mili.com; Michalská 21; ⊙ 2-7pm Mon-Fri; Ⓜ Můstek)

Botanicus
BEAUTY

25 🔒 Map p78, D1

Prepare for olfactory overload in this always-busy outlet for natural health and beauty products. The scented soaps, herbal bath oils and shampoos, fruit cordials and handmade paper products are made using herbs and plants grown on an or-

Understand

Literary Prague

Prague has a well-deserved reputation as a literary heavyweight. The names Franz Kafka and Milan Kundera will be familiar to any serious reader, but Prague's writing roots run deeper – it's no accident the country's first postcommunist president, Václav Havel, was a playwright. In addition to its Czech writers, the city was also once a hotbed of German literature.

Czech Literary Lights

Besides the clever Kundera (b 1929), Prague was home to humourist Bohumil Hrabal (1914–97), whose many books are widely translated into English. The film based on his novel *Closely Watched Trains* won the Oscar for Best Foreign Film in 1968. Another near-household name is Jaroslav Hašek (1883–1923), whose book *The Good Soldier Švejk* is a stroke of comic genius along the lines of *Catch-22*. Czech poet Jaroslav Seifert won the Nobel Prize for poetry in 1984.

The German Connection

In the 19th and early 20th centuries, Prague was a centre of German literature. Kafka (1883–1924), a German-speaking Jewish writer, remains the gold standard: his books *The Trial* and *The Castle*, among many others, are modern classics. But Prague was also home to Kafka's friend and publisher Max Brod (1883–1924), as well as noted writers Egon Erwin Kisch (1885–1948) and Franz Werfel (1890–1945). One of the most beloved poets in the German language, Rainer Maria Rilke (1875–1926), was born and studied in Prague.

New Voices

There's no shortage of new Czech literary talent: Jáchym Topol (b 1962), Petra Hůlová (b 1979), Michal Viewegh (b 1962), Michal Ajvaz (b 1949), Emil Hakl (b 1958) and Miloš Urban (b 1967) are taking their places among the country's leading authors. They're pushing out old-guard figures, now seen as chroniclers of a very different, postcommunist age. Until recently, few books from these younger novelists had been translated into English. That's changing slowly, however, as publishers appear more willing to take a chance on marketing them to English-speaking audiences.

ganic farm at Ostrá, east of Prague. (☎ 234 767 446; www.botanicus.cz; Týn 3; ⏰10am-6.30pm; Ⓜ Náměstí Republiky)

Manufaktura ARTS & CRAFTS

26 🔒 Map p78, C2

There are several Manufaktura outlets across town, but this small branch near the Old Town Square seems to keep its inventory especially enticing. You'll find great Czech wooden toys, beautiful-looking (if extremely chewy) honey gingerbread made from elaborate medieval moulds, and seasonal gifts such as hand-painted Easter eggs. (☎ 257 533 678; www.manufaktura.cz; Melantrichova 17; ⏰10am-8pm; Ⓜ Můstek)

Modernista HOMEWARES

Modernista specialises in reproduction 20th-century furniture, ceramics, glassware and jewellery, in classic styles ranging from art deco and cubist to functionalist and Bauhaus – including sensuously curved chairs that are a feature of the Icon Hotel, and an unusual chaise lounge by Adolf Loos. The shop is in the information centre at the Municipal House (see **1** ◉ Map p78, E2). (☎ 224 241 300; www. modernista.cz; Obecní dům, náměstí Republiky 5; ⏰11am-6pm; Ⓜ Náměstí Republiky)

Material GLASS

27 🔒 Map p78, D1

Material puts a modern twist on the Czech crystal industry, with its oversized contemporary vases, bowls and Dale Chihuly–like ornaments, candleholders, chandeliers and glasses. The firm boasts its 'drunken sailor' glass is spillproof. Yet, despite well-spaced displays, it's a store where you immediately fear breaking something –

Understand
The Trials of Tycho Brahe

It's probably more than fair to describe Tycho Brahe, who's buried in the Church of Our Lady Before Týn (p75), as something of a character. This Danish father of modern astronomy catalogued thousands of stars, made stunningly accurate observations in an era before telescopes, and helped his assistant Johannes Kepler derive the laws of planetary motion.

He came to Prague in 1599 as Emperor Rudolf II's official mathematician. But Brahe also dabbled in astrology and alchemy. He lost part of his nose in a duel and wore a metal replacement. His pet moose apparently drank too much beer, fell down the stairs and died.

In Prague, Brahe himself died in 1601 of a bladder infection, reputedly because he was too polite to go to the toilet during a long banquet. Only recently have historians decided he was probably poisoned instead. We're not sure which version is more comforting.

Old Town Square (p74) and Church of Our Lady Before Týn (p75)

and when you check the prices you realise you should! (📞608 664 766; www.i-material.com; Týn 1; ⏱10.30am-8pm; Ⓜ Náměstí Republiky)

Pohádka   TOYS

28 🔒 Map p78, D2

This store is sometimes beset by souvenir-hunting tour groups and it stocks plenty of *matryoshky* (Russian stacking dolls) – objects that actually have nothing to do with Prague. Surprisingly, then, it's also a pretty-good place to shop for genuine Czech toys, from marionettes and costumed dolls to finger puppets, rocking horses and toy cars. (📞224 239 469; www.czechtoys. cz; Celetná 32; ⏱9am-8pm; Ⓜ Náměstí Republiky)

Explore

Wenceslas Square & Around

Busy Wenceslas Square, dating from 1348 and once a bustling horse market, was the site of several seminal events in Czech history. Today, though it's crowded with souvenir shops, clubs, coffee chains and plenty of tourists, it's possible to glimpse the square's previous grandeur simply by looking up at the glorious art nouveau architecture.

The Sights in a Day

☀️ Start the day at the bottom of **Wenceslas Square** (p92), the most important part of Nové Město. The square is a hodgepodge of architectural styles, but the art nouveau facade of the **Grand Hotel Evropa** (p93) stands out. Walk up the square at your leisure, popping in to the **Hotel Jalta** (p95) to see an underground nuclear bunker. Check out the **Wenceslas Statue** (p93), the square's focal point. The National Museum is closed for renovation, but you can still take in the view, and also pay your respects at the **Jan Palach Memorial** (p93) and gaze over at the former headquarters of **Radio Free Europe** (p93).

☀️ For lunch, head north of the square for standard pub fare at **U Ferdinanda** (p99), which then puts you within easy walking distance for the **Mucha Museum** (p95) to admire the painter's dreamlike beauties emblazoned on early-20th-century Parisian posters.

🌙 For dinner, try some amazing tapas at **Room** (p97) or go totally casual for ribs and a Czech regional beer at **Jáma** (p99). If you want something dressier, try **Kogo** (p99) and then a night of ballet or opera at the **Prague State Opera** (p100).

👁️ **Top Sights**

Wenceslas Square (p92)

💜 **Best of Prague**

Food
Room (p97)
Kogo (p99)

Museums
Mucha Museum (p95)
Museum of Communism (p96)

Architecture
Grand Hotel Evropa (p93)

Shopping
Moser (p101)
Baťa (p101)

Culture
State Opera House (p100)
Kino Světozor (p100)

Nightlife
Lucerna Music Bar (p100)

Getting There

Ⓜ **Metro** Lines A and B cross at Můstek at the bottom of the square. Lines A and C meet at Muzeum at the top.

Top Sights
Wenceslas Square

This massive central square was founded by Charles IV in 1348. For hundreds of years it was called the 'Horse Market' and featured a small lake, horse-drawn trams and the first Czech theatre. In medieval times it was also the site of several public executions. On 28 October 1918, the independent republic of Czechoslovakia was announced here; in 1945 the end of WWII was declared and celebrated. Later, during the Velvet Revolution, the square hosted huge, historic demonstrations.

Map p94, C3

Václavské náměstí

M Můstek, Muzeum

St Wenceslas Statue

Don't Miss

Jan Palach Memorial
In January 1969 university student Jan Palach set fire to himself in front of the National Museum to protest against the Soviet-led invasion of Czechoslovakia the preceding August. Palach later died from his wounds and became a national hero. The memorial sits at the exact spot where Palach fell, marked by a cross in the pavement just below the steps to the museum's entrance.

Former Radio Free Europe Building
During the Cold War, many Czechs and Slovaks turned to US-financed Radio Free Europe for news from the West. After 1989, the radio moved its headquarters from Munich here to the former Czechoslovak Federal Parliament building (at the top of the square, just to the left of the National Museum). In 2008, RFE moved to a new building in the Prague suburbs, and the old headquarters is now used as a National Museum annex.

St Wenceslas Statue
The focal point of Wenceslas Square is the equestrian statue of St Wenceslas at its southern end. Sculptor Josef Myslbek has surrounded the 10th-century Duke of Bohemia (and 'Good King Wenceslas' of Christmas-carol fame) with four other patron saints of Bohemia – Prokop, Adalbert, Agnes and Ludmila.

Grand Hotel Evropa
Grand indeed – this ornate art nouveau hotel and cafe at Václavské náměstí 25 is easily the most colourful building on a colourful square. Unfortunately, it was closed for renovation at the time of writing and it wasn't clear when it would reopen.

EDDIE GERALD/ALAMY ©

☑ Top Tips
▶ During holidays and festivals, try the square's food and drink stands for local specialities like spiced wine and grilled sausage.

▶ Keep an eye on your belongings, especially at night – this area is notorious for pickpockets and touts.

▶ Many restaurants on the square are tourist traps; better-value options are nearby.

✗ Take a Break
To escape the throngs, dive into the Lucerna shopping passage on Wenceslas Square's southern side (enter from either Vodičkova or Štěpánská). Two cafes great for a quick coffee are the elegant, 1920s-style **Kavárna Lucerna** (www.restaurace-monarchie.cz; Lucerna Pasáž, Štěpánská 61; ⊙10am-midnight), on the upper floor, and the student favourite, **Kávovarna** (Pasáž Lucerna, Štěpánská 61; ⊙8am-midnight), on the ground floor.

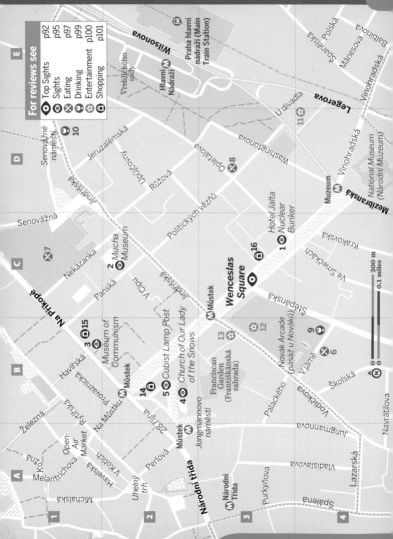

Senovážné náměstí

Wilsonova

Praha hlavní nádraží (Main Train Station)

Ⓚ

Hlavní Ⓜ Nádraží

Vrchlického sady

Legerova

Španělská

Polská

Balbínova

Mánesova

Vinohradská

U divadla

11 ✪

Washingtonova

Opletalova

Jindřišská

Jeruzalémská

Růžová

Senovážná

Politických vězňů

9⃣ 10

Senovážné náměstí

Jindřišská

Vinohradská

National Museum (Národní Muzeum)

Hotel Jalta

1 ◉ Nuclear Bunker

Muzeum Ⓜ

Mezibranská

Krakovská

Ve Smečkách

7 ✖

Nekázanka

Panská

V Cípu

2 ◉ Mucha Museum

16 ⌂

Wenceslas Square

◉

Štěpánská

Na Příkopě

Havířská

Museum of Communism

3⃣ 15

Ⓜ Můstek

Jindřišská

Můstek Ⓜ

13 ✪

Franciscan Garden (Františkánská zahrada)

12 ✪

Nové Arcade (pasáž u Nováků)

9⃣

V Jámě

6 ✖

Školská

Palackého

Vodičkova

Jungmannova

Štěpánská

Navrátilova

200 m
0.1 miles

Ⓜ

Železná

Rytířská

Provaznická

14 ⌂

Ⓜ Můstek

Na Můstku

28. října

Perlová

5 ◉ Cubist Lamp Post

4 ◉ Church of Our Lady of the Snows

Jungmannovo náměstí

Ⓜ Můstek

Vladislavova

Lazarská

Spálená

Michalská

Kožná

Melantrichova

Open-Air Market

Havelská

V kotcích

Uhelný trh

Národní třída

Ⓜ Národní Třída

Purkyňova

Navrátilova

Sights

Hotel Jalta
Nuclear Bunker   HISTORIC BUILDING

1 ◉ Map p94, C3

Hidden beneath the 1950s Hotel Jalta on Wenceslas Square lies a communist-era nuclear shelter that was opened to the public in 2013. The tour (in Czech, with an English text), led by a guide in period security-police uniform, takes in a series of secret chambers; the highlight is the comms room, where wiretaps in the bedrooms of important guests were monitored. (☏ 222 822 111; www.hoteljalta. com; Václavské náměstí 45; per person 75Kč; ⊗ 5-8pm Mon & Wed even weeks, Tue & Thu odd weeks; M Muzeum)

Mucha Museum   GALLERY

2 ◉ Map p94, C2

This fascinating (and busy) museum features the sensuous art nouveau posters, paintings and decorative panels of Alfons Mucha (1860–1939), as well as many sketches, photographs and other memorabilia. The exhibits include countless artworks showing Mucha's trademark Slavic maidens with flowing hair and piercing blue eyes, bearing symbolic garlands and linden boughs. (Muchovo muzuem; ☏ 221 451 333; www.mucha.cz; Panská 7; adult/child 240/140Kč; ⊗ 10am-6pm; M Můstek)

Understand
Overhaul of the National Museum

The National Museum, at the top end of the square, dates from the last half of the 19th century, when bombastic architecture was all the rage. The style, neo-Renaissance, was meant as a conscious aping of the Renaissance palaces that were built around Prague in the 16th century. The grand size served two purposes: the museum's vast holdings could finally fit under one roof, and the building was meant to symbolise the power of the growing Czech (as opposed to Austrian or German) elite.

As this book was being written, the museum was undergoing long-term renovation – until 2015 at the earliest. The repairs are meant to spruce up the facade (which was still sporting bullet holes from 1968, when it was fired on by invading Russian troops who mistook it for Parliament) and to modernise the fusty exhibits of fossils, rocks and bones. During the renovation, the museum is organising temporary exhibits next door at the **National Museum's new building** (☏ 224 497 111; www.nm.cz; Vinohradská 1; adult/child 110/75Kč; ⊗ 10am-6pm; M Muzeum).

Museum of Communism

MUSEUM

3 ⊙ Map p94, B1

It's difficult to think of a more ironic site for a museum of communism – in an 18th-century aristocrat's palace, between a casino on one side and a McDonald's on the other. Put together by an American expat and his Czech partner, the museum tells the story of Czechoslovakia's years behind the Iron Curtain in photos, words and a fascinating and varied collection of...well, stuff. (Muzeum Komunismu; ☎224 212 966; www.muzeum komunismu.cz; Na Příkopě 10; adult/child under 10/concession 190/free/150Kč; ⊙9am-9pm; ⓜMůstek)

Church of Our Lady of the Snows

CHURCH

4 ⊙ Map p94, B2

This Gothic church at the northern end of Wenceslas Square was begun in the 14th century by Charles IV, but only the chancel was ever completed, which accounts for its proportions – seemingly taller than it is long. Charles had intended it to be the grandest church in Prague; the nave is higher than that of St Vitus Cathedral, and the altar is the city's tallest.

Understand
Much Ado About Mucha

Alfons Mucha (1860–1939) is the Czech answer to Austria's Gustav Klimt, England's William Morris or Scotland's Charles Rennie Mackintosh.

One of the fathers – if not *the* father – of art nouveau as represented in the visual arts, he first found fame in Paris after producing a stunning poster for actress Sarah Bernhardt's 1895 play *Gismonda*. A contract with Bernhardt, reams of advertising work and trips to America brought him international renown.

Mucha returned home in 1909, and went on to design the banknotes for the first Czechoslovak Republic after 1918. Around this time, he also produced his opus, a collection of 20 gigantic canvases telling the history of the Slavic peoples, which he titled the *Slav Epic* (*Slovanská epopej*).

Mucha created some of the stunning interiors of Prague's Municipal House (p79) and designed a beautiful stained-glass window for St Vitus Cathedral (p30). His signature art nouveau work is on display at the Mucha Museum (p95).

Long-held plans to exhibit the *Slav Epic* in Prague came to fruition in 2013, when the canvases were put on display at the National Gallery's Veletržní palác (p126); they're slated to stay through at least 2015.

Alfons Mucha posters on display in Prague

(Kostel Panny Marie Sněžné; www.pms.ofm.
cz; Jungmannovo náměstí 18; M̄ Můstek)

Cubist Lamp Post ART

5 Map p94, B2

Angular but slightly chunky, made
from striated concrete – the world's
only cubist lamp post would be worth
going out of the way to see. So it's
a happy bonus that this novelty is
just conveniently located just around
the corner from Wenceslas Square.
(Jungmannovo náměstí; M̄ Můstek)

Eating

Room SPANISH €€

6 Map p94, B4

Cool, angular and precise in shades
of grey, black and avocado green,
Room provides the perfect setting
for some of Prague's most carefully
crafted flavours. With an accomplished kitchen team working from
a menu created by actor Tommy Lee
Jones' personal chef, it's no surprise
that the food – *gambas pil pil* (garlic
prawns), clams and chorizo in cider,

Understand

Oppression & Revolution

From Coup to Invasion

February 1948 marked the start of a half-century's worth of political turmoil in Prague. It was at this time that the leaders of the Czechoslovak Communist Party (KSČ), not content with a controlling position in the postwar coalition after the 1946 elections, staged a coup backed by the Soviet Union. The next two decades saw widespread political persecution.

In the late 1960s, Communist Party leader Alexander Dubček loosened the reins slightly under the banner 'Socialism With a Human Face'. There was a resurgence in literature, theatre and film, led by the likes of Milan Kundera, Bohumil Hrabal, Václav Havel and Miloš Forman. The Soviet regime crushed this 'Prague Spring' on 20 and 21 August 1968, using Warsaw Pact tanks, and Dubček was replaced by hardliner Gustáv Husák.

The Fall of Communism

The Husák government expelled many reform communists from positions of authority and introduced what Czechs called 'normalisation' – in other words, Soviet-style repression. Active dissent was limited to a few hundred people, mostly intellectuals and artists, including playwright Václav Havel.

In November 1989, as communist regimes tumbled across Eastern Europe, the Czechoslovak government came under increasing pressure to relinquish power. On 17 November, riot police cracked down on a peaceful student protest march, which would prove to be the catalyst to revolution. Within days, crowds on Wenceslas Square swelled to some 500,000 people.

A group led by Havel procured the government's resignation on 3 December, and 26 days later, he was the new leader. The 'Velvet Revolution' – named for its peaceful nature (as well as the inspiration its leaders took from the rock band the Velvet Underground) – had triumphed.

A Velvet Divorce

The transition to democracy was anything but smooth, though it eventually succeeded. Ironically, one casualty of the revolution was the splitting of the country into separate Czech and Slovak states in 1993. The amicable breakup later became known as the 'Velvet Divorce'.

oxtail with parsnip purée – is top-notch. (📞221 634 103; www.tapasroom.cz; Icon Hotel, V Jámě 6; tapas 50-320Kc, mains 230-400Kč; ⏱7am-1am; 📶; 🚋3, 9, 14, 24)

Kogo

ITALIAN €€

7 Map p94, C1

Chic and businesslike, but also relaxed and family friendly (highchairs provided), Kogo is a stylish restaurant serving top-notch pizza, pasta, and Italian meat and seafood dishes – the rich, tomatoey *zuppa di pesce* (fish soup) is delicious, as is the *risotto alla pescatora* (with squid, mussels, shrimp and octopus). On summer evenings, candlelit tables filled with conversation spill over into the leafy courtyard. (📞221 451 259; www.kogo.cz; Slovanský dům, Na Příkopě 22; mains 250-680Kč; ⏱11am-11pm; 📶♿; Ⓜ Náměstí Republiky)

U Ferdinanda

CZECH €

8 Map p94, D3

Welcome to a thoroughly modern spin on a classic Czech pub, with beer courtesy of the Ferdinand brewery from nearby Benešov. Quirky gardening implements in corrugated iron decorate the raucous interior, and a younger local clientele crowds in for well-priced Czech food. (📞222 244 302; www.ferdinanda.cz; cnr ulice Opletalova & Politických Vězňů; mains 100-180Kč; ⏱11am-11pm Mon-Sat; Ⓜ Muzeum)

Drinking

Jáma

BAR

9 Map p94, B4

Jáma ('the Hollow') is a popular American-expat bar plastered with old music-gig posters ranging from Led Zep and REM to Kiss and Shania Twain. There's a little beer garden out the back shaded by lime and walnut trees, smiling staff serving up a rotating selection of regional beers and microbrews, and a menu that includes good burgers, steaks, ribs and chicken wings. (📞222 967 081; www.jamapub.cz; V Jámě 7; ⏱11am-1am; 📶; Ⓜ Muzeum)

Hoffa

COCKTAIL BAR

10 Map p94, D1

One of Prague's first entirely smoke-free bars, Hoffa matches clean air with clean design: a long (12m!) bar fronting a long room with sleek, functional decor, and a wall of windows looking out onto Senovážné náměstí's fountain of dancing sprites. Friendly staff, accomplished cocktails and good snacks – there's even homemade lemonade and iced tea at lunchtime. (📞601 359 659; www.hoffa.cz; Senovážné náměstí 22; ⏱11am-2am Mon-Fri, 6pm-2am Sat & Sun; 📶; 🚋5, 9, 26)

Entertainment

Prague State Opera
OPERA, DANCE

11 ⭐ Map p94, D4

The impressive neo-rococo home of the Prague State Opera provides a glorious setting for performances of opera and ballet. An annual Verdi festival takes place here in August and September, and less conventional shows, such as Leoncavallo's rarely staged version of *La Bohème,* are also performed here. (Státní opera Praha; ☎224 901 448; www.narodni-divadlo.cz; Wilsonova 4; tickets 180-1190Kč; ⊙box office 10am-6pm; Ⓜ Muzeum)

Lucerna Music Bar
LIVE MUSIC

12 ⭐ Map p94, B3

Nostalgia reigns supreme at this atmospheric old theatre, now looking a little dog-eared, which hosts a hugely popular 1980s and '90s video party every Friday and Saturday night, with crowds of young locals bopping along to Duran Duran and Gary Numan. There's an impressively eclectic program of live bands on midweek nights, with everything from Slovakian ska and Belgian pop-rock to Dutch electro-funk and American metal. (☎224 217 108; www.musicbar.cz; Palác Lucerna, Vodičkova 36; cover 100-500Kč; ⊙8pm-4am; Ⓜ Můstek)

Kino Světozor
CINEMA

13 ⭐ Map p94, B3

The Světozor is under the same management as Žižkov's famous **Kino Aero** (☎271 771 349; www.kinoaero.cz; Biskupcova 31, Žižkov; tickets 60-110Kč; 🛜; 🚃9, 10, 11, 16), but is more central, and has the same emphasis on classic cinema, documentary and art-house films screened in their original language – everything from *Battleship Potemkin* and *Casablanca* to *Annie*

Understand
Prague's Grand Cafes

Prague is known for pubs, Vienna for its coffee houses. Yet the Czech capital also boasts grand cafes that rival their Austrian cousins in looks (even if the actual coffee can't compete). At least the atmosphere is equivalent, and since the days of the Austro-Hungarian Empire onwards, Prague's ornate, high-ceilinged coffee houses have acted as public meeting spaces, hotbeds of political subversion and literary salons.

At various times Franz Kafka, playwright Karel Čapek (coiner of the term 'robot') and Albert Einstein all drank at Cafe Louvre (p106), while across the road at Kavárna Slavia (p106), patrons included Milan Kundera, Václav Havel and other writers, playwrights and filmmakers.

Hall and *The Motorcycle Diaries* – plus critically acclaimed box-office hits. (📞224 946 824; www.kinosvetozor. cz; Vodičkova 41; tickets 60-120Kč; 🛜; Ⓜ Můstek)

Shopping

Baťa
SHOES

14 Map p94, B2

Established by Tomáš Baťa in 1894, the Baťa footwear empire is still in family hands and is one of the Czech Republic's most successful companies. The flagship store on Wenceslas Square, built in the 1920s, is considered a masterpiece of modern architecture, and houses six floors of shoes (including international brands as well as Baťa's own), handbags, luggage and leather goods. (📞221 088 478; www.bata. cz; Václavské náměstí 6; 🕘9am-9pm Mon-Fri, 9am-8pm Sat, 10am-8pm Sun; Ⓜ Můstek)

Moser
GLASS

15 Map p94, B1

One of the most exclusive and respected of Bohemian glassmakers, Moser was founded in Karlovy Vary in 1857 and is famous for its rich and flamboyant designs. The shop on Na Příkopě is worth a browse as much for the decor as for the goods – it's in a magnificently decorated, originally Gothic building called the House of the Black Rose (dům U černé růže). (📞224 211 293; www.moser-glass.com; Na Příkopě 12; 🕘10am-8pm; Ⓜ Můstek)

🔍 Local Life
Shopping 'At the Moat'

Crossing the lower end of Wenceslas Square, Na Příkopě is one of the city's prettiest and most popular promenades. The name translates as 'At the Moat' – the street traces a moat that once ran between Staré Město and Nové Město to protect the Old Town from attack.

In the 19th century, Na Příkopě was the fashionable haunt of Austrian cafe society. Today, it's typical high-street shopping turf, lined with international retail chains like H&M, Mango and Zara, and dotted with colourful shopping malls, including dům U černé růže (House of the Black Rose) at No 12, **Myslbek pasáž** (www.myslbek.com) at No 21, Slovanský dům at No 22, and **Palladium** (www.palladiumpraha. cz) at náměstí Republiky 1.

Palác Knih Neo Luxor
BOOKS

16 Map p94, C3

Palác Knih Neo Luxor is Prague's biggest bookshop – head for the basement to find a wide selection of fiction and nonfiction in English, German, French and Russian, including Czech authors in translation. You'll also find internet access, a cafe and a good selection of international newspapers and magazines. (📞296 110 368; www. neoluxor.cz; Václavské náměstí 41; 🕘8am-8pm Mon-Fri, 9am-7pm Sat, 10am-7pm Sun; Ⓜ Muzeum)

Explore

Nové Město

Nové Město is a long, arching neighbourhood that borders Staré Město on its eastern and southern edges. The name translates as 'New Town', which is something of a misnomer since the area was established nearly 700 years ago by Emperor Charles IV. But unlike Staré Město or Malá Strana, the historic feeling is missing here, owing mainly to massive rebuilding in the 19th century.

The Sights in a Day

☀ Start your day with a cup of coffee at **Kavárna Slavia** (p106) – try to snag a river-facing table with a view to Prague Castle. Meander down by the river, heading south to **Slav Island** (p105), where you can rent a paddle boat and enjoy a terrific, water-level view of Charles Bridge. From here, wander further south to take in the **Dancing Building** (pictured left; p105), designed by Vlado Milunić and Frank Gehry, one of the few modern buildings in Prague to make a splash in architectural circles. From there, head east to the **Church of Sts Cyril & Methodius** (p106), the site of a dramatic stand-off between the Nazis and a band of brave Czechoslovak paratroopers during World War II (p106).

☀ Follow Na Zderace north to a quieter part of town, the area south of Národní třída. Grab a spicy Thai lunch at **Lemon Leaf** (p105) or soup and sandwich combo at the **Globe Bookstore & Cafe** (p105).

☾ In the evening get tickets to see a ballet or opera at the beautiful **National Theatre** (p107) or enjoy a jazz set at **Reduta** (p107). Kids will enjoy a night of 'black theatre' at **Laterna Magika** (p108). **Cafe Louvre** (p106), though technically a coffee house, is a terrific choice for a stylish Czech dinner.

 Best of Prague

Food
Globe Bookstore & Café (p105)

Lemon Leaf (p105)

History
National Memorial to the Heroes of the Heydrich Terror (p106)

Architecture
Dancing Building (p105)

Culture
National Theatre (p107)

Laterna Magika (p108)

Drinking
Cafe Louvre (p106)

Kavárna Slavia (p106)

Pivovarský Dům (p107)

Music
Reduta Jazz Club (p107)

Jazz Republic (p108)

Getting There

Ⓜ **Metro** Line B to Můstek or Karlovo Náměstí; Line A to Můstek.

🚊 **Tram** Trams 6, 9, 17, 18, 22 to Národní divadlo.

200 m
0.1 miles

For reviews see
- ◎ Sights — p105
- ✕ Eating — p105
- 🍷 Drinking — p106
- ★ Entertainment — p107
- 🛍 Shopping — p109

Mezibranská

Ⓜ Muzeum

Krakovská

Ve Smečkách

Wenceslas
Square
(Václavské
náměstí)

Štěpánská

Lucerna Palace
(Palác Lucerna)

V jámě

Ⓜ Můstek

Franciscan Garden
(Františkánská
zahrada)

Jungmannovo
náměstí

Školská

Vodičkova

Palackého

Řeznická

Navrátilova

Na Rybníčku II

Žitná

Ječná

Lípová

Jungmannova

Ⓜ Můstek

Adria
Palace

Vladislavova

Lazarská

Příčná

Malá Štěpánská

Charles
Square
(Karlovo
náměstí)

Charles
Square
(Karlovo
náměstí)

Ⓜ Národní
Třída

Purkyňova

Spálená

**NOVÉ
MĚSTO**

**NOVÉ
MĚSTO**

Na Perštýně

◎ 5

◎ 6
◎ 11
🛍 14

Mikulandská

Ostrovní

V Jirchářích

Černá

Ⓜ Karlovo
Náměstí

Odborů

Vyšehradská

Václavská

Národní třída

Voršilská

Opatovická

Křemencová

✕ 8

Myslíkova

✕ 3

✕ 4

Na Zderaze

Resslova

Dittrichova

Divadelní

Bartolomějská

Konviktská

Pštrossova

Na struze

Vojtěšská

Šítkova

Zlatnická

🛍 13

Smetanovo nábřeží

★ 7

◎ 10

Masarykovo nábřeží

Slav
Island

Slav Island
(Slovanský
ostrov)

◎ 2

Jirásek
Square
(Jiráskovo
náměstí)

Dancing
Building

◎ 1

Jirásek
Bridge
(Jiráskův
most)

IP Pavlova

Kateřinská

◎ 9

Sights

Dancing Building   ARCHITECTURE

1 Map p104, A4

The Dancing Building was built in 1996 by architects Vlado Milunić and Frank Gehry. The curved lines of the narrow-waisted glass tower clutched against its more upright and formal partner led to it being christened the 'Fred & Ginger' building, after legendary dancing duo Fred Astaire and Ginger Rogers. It's surprising how well it fits in with its ageing neighbours. (Tančící dům; www.tancici-dum.cz; Rašínovo nábřeží 80; ⛴14, 17)

Slav Island   ISLAND

2 Map p104, A2

This island is a sleepy, dog-eared sandbank with pleasant gardens, river views and several jetties where you can hire rowing boats. In the middle stands **Žofín**, a 19th-century cultural centre that has been restored and opened as a restaurant and social venue. In 1925 the island was named after the Slav conventions that had taken place here since 1848. (Slovanský ostrov; Masarykovo nábřeží; ⛴17, 21)

Eating

Globe Bookstore & Café   CAFE €

3 Map p104, B3

This appealing expat bookshop-cafe serves nachos, burgers, chicken wings and salads until 11pm nightly, and also offers an excellent brunch menu (from 9.30am to 4pm Saturday and Sunday) that includes an American classic (bacon, egg and hash browns), full English fry-up, blueberry pancakes and freshly squeezed juices. Lighter breakfasts are served from 9.30am to 11.30am weekdays. (☎224 934 203; www.globebookstore.cz; Pštrossova 6; mains 160-200Kč; ⏱9.30am-midnight, to 1am Fri & Sat; 🛜; Ⓜ Karlovo Náměstí)

Lemon Leaf   ASIAN €

4 Map p104, B3

It's a bit off the beaten tourist path, but with its bright, high-ceiling rooms decked out with crushed-silk lampshades and Thai-style art, the Lemon Leaf is certainly making an effort to pull in the visitors. It's worth a visit for excellent, authentic Thai dishes, including a rich and fragrant green curry with a decent kick of chilli heat. (☎224 919 056; www.lemon.cz; Myslíkova 14; mains 179-209Kč; ⏱11am-11pm; 🛜; ⛴14)

Pho Viet   VIETNAMESE €

5 Map p104, B1

Tucked away in the far corner of a shopping arcade, this unassuming little place serves up fresh *nem tuoi* (prawn rolls) and aromatic *pho* (beef and noodle soup with coriander) with searingly hot chillis. No prizes for decor – think workers' canteen – but the price:tastiness ratio can't be beat. (☎777 724 489; Národní třída 25; mains 60-90Kč; ⏱10am-11pm; Ⓜ Národní Třída)

Drinking

Cafe Louvre
CAFE

 6 Map p104, B1

Others are more famous, but the French-style Louvre is arguably Prague's most amenable grand cafe. The atmosphere is wonderfully 'olde worlde', but there's a proper nonsmoking section among its warren of rooms and it serves good coffee, as well as food. Pop in for breakfast, play a little billiards and check out the associated art gallery downstairs when leaving.

(224 930 949; www.cafelouvre.cz; 1st fl, Národní třída 22; 6, 9, 18, 22)

Kavárna Slavia
CAFE

7 Map p104, A1

The Slavia is the most famous of Prague's old cafés, a cherrywood-and-onyx shrine to art deco elegance, with polished-limestone-topped tables and big windows overlooking the river. It has been a celebrated literary meeting place since the early 20th century – Rainer Maria Rilke and Franz Kafka hung out here, and it was frequented by Václav Havel

---

Understand

Heroic Paratroopers

In 1941, during World War II, the occupying Nazi government appointed SS general Reinhard Heydrich, Hitler's heir apparent, as Reichsprotektor of Bohemia and Moravia. The move came in response to a series of crippling strikes and sabotage operations by the Czech resistance movement, and Heydrich immediately cracked down with a vengeance.

In an effort to support the resistance and boost Czech morale, Britain secretly trained a team of Czechoslovak paratroopers to assassinate Heydrich. The daring mission was code-named 'Operation Anthropoid' – and against all odds it succeeded. On 27 May 1942, two paratroopers, Jan Kubiš and Jozef Gabčík, attacked Heydrich as he rode in his official car through the city's Libeň district; he later died from the wounds.

The assassins and five co-conspirators fled but were betrayed in their hiding place in the Church of Sts Cyril & Methodius; all seven died in the ensuing siege. This moving story is told at the **National Memorial to the Heroes of the Heydrich Terror** (Národní památník hrdinů Heydrichiády; 224 916 100; www.pamatnik-heydrichiady.cz; Resslova 9; adult/concession 75/35Kč; 9am-5pm Tue-Sun Mar-Oct, 9am-5pm Tue-Sat Nov-Feb; M Karlovo Náměstí) located at the church.

The Nazis reacted with a frenzied wave of terror, which included the annihilation of two entire Czech villages, Ležáky and Lidice, and the shattering of the underground movement.

and other dissidents in the 1970s and '80s. (☎224 220 957; www.cafeslavia.cz; Národní třída 1; ☺8am-midnight Mon-Fri, 9am-midnight Sat & Sun; 🛜; 🚃6, 9, 12, 20, 22)

U Fleků   BREWERY

8 Map p104, B3

A festive warren of drinking and dining rooms, U Fleků is a Prague institution, though usually clogged with tour groups high on oompah music and the tavern's home-brewed, 13° black beer (59Kč for 0.4L), known as Flek. Purists grumble but go along anyway because the beer is good, though tourist prices have nudged out many locals. (☎224 934 019; www.ufleku. cz; Křemencová 11; ☺10am-11pm; Ⓜ Karlovo Náměstí)

Pivovarský Dům   BREWERY

9 Map p104, D4

Locals gather here to sample the classic Czech lager (44Kč per 0.5L) that is produced on the premises, as well as wheat beer and a range of flavoured beers (including coffee, banana and cherry, 44Kč per 0.3L). The pub itself is a pleasant place to linger, decked out with polished copper vats and brewing implements, and smelling faintly of malt and hops. (☎296 216 666; www.pivovarskydum. com; cnr Ječná & Lípová; ☺11am-11.30pm; 🚃4, 10, 16, 22)

Entertainment

National Theatre   OPERA, BALLET

10 Map p104, A2

The much-loved National Theatre provides a stage for traditional opera, drama and ballet by the likes of Smetana, Shakespeare and Tchaikovsky, alongside more modern works by composers and playwrights such as Philip Glass and John Osborne. The box offices are in the Nový síň building next door, in the Kolowrat Palace (opposite the Estates Theatre) and at the State Opera. (Národní divadlo; ☎224 901 448; www.narodni-divadlo.cz; Národní třída 2; tickets 50-1100Kč; ☺box offices 10am-6pm; 🚃6, 9, 18, 22)

Reduta Jazz Club   JAZZ

11 Map p104, B1

The Reduta is Prague's oldest jazz club, founded in 1958 during the communist era – it was here in 1994 that then US president Bill Clinton famously jammed on a new saxophone presented to him by Václav Havel. It has an intimate setting, with smartly dressed patrons squeezing into tiered seats and lounges to soak up the big band, swing and Dixieland atmosphere. (☎224 933 487; www.reduta jazzclub.cz; Národní třída 20; cover 330Kč; ☺9pm-3am; 🛜; Ⓜ Národní Třída)

Jazz Republic

LIVE MUSIC

12 ⭐ Map p104, C1

Despite the name, this relaxed club stages all kinds of live music, including rock, blues, reggae and fusion as well as jazz. Bands are mostly local, and the music is not overpowering – you can easily hold a conversation –

Ⓠ Local Life
South of Národní Třída

The area south of Národní třída, behind the National Theatre, is lined with lesser-known ethnic eateries, student-populated cafes, and (lots of) bars. It's lovely part of town to wander along as the sun fades. Come back after dark, since this is one of the better places to party.

The **Red Room** (☎222 520 084; www.redroom.cz; Myslíkova 28; ⏱6pm-1am Tue-Thu, 6pm-2am Fri, 7pm-2am Sat, 7pm-1am Sun; 🛜; 🚋14 to Myslíkova, Ⓜ Karlovo Náměstí) is a laid-back bar stuffed with friendly expats and offering occasional live music.

Kavárna Velryba (☎224 931 444; www.kavarnavelryba.cz; Opatovická 24; ⏱11am-midnight Sun-Thu, to 2am Fri; 🛜; 🚌6, 9, 18, 22 to Národní třída) is an arty cafe-bar with vegetarian-friendly snacks, a smoky back room and a basement art gallery.

Head to **Bokovka** (☎222 544 014; www.bokovka.com; Pštrossova 8; ⏱4pm-1am Mon-Sat; 🛜; Ⓜ Karlovo Náměstí) for an extensive menu of top-notch Moravian wines and welcoming nonsmoking ambience.

which means it won't please the purists (ssssh!). The entrance is at the foot of the stairs leading down to Můstek metro station. (☎224 282 235; www.jazzrepublic.cz; 28.října 1; tickets 100Kč; ⏱5pm-late, music from 9pm)

Laterna Magika

PERFORMING ARTS

13 ⭐ Map p104, A2

Laterna Magika has been wowing audiences since its first cutting-edge multimedia show caused a stir at the 1958 Brussels World Fair. Its imaginative blend of dance, music and projected images continues to pull in the crowds. Nová Scena, the futuristic building next to the National Theatre, has been home to Laterna Magika since it moved from its birthplace in the Adria Palace in the mid-1970s. (☎224 901 448; www.narodni-divadlo.cz; Nová Scéna, Národní třída 4; tickets 260-690Kč; ⏱box office 9am-6pm Mon-Fri, 10am-6pm Sat & Sun; 🚋6, 9, 18, 22)

Rock Café

LIVE MUSIC

Not to be confused with the Hard Rock Café, this multifunction club (see **11** ⭐ Map p104, B1) is the offspring of the influential Nový Horizont art movement of the 1990s. It sports a stage for DJs and live rock bands, a funkily decorated 'rock cafe', a cinema, a theatre, an art gallery and a CD shop. Live bands are mostly local, ranging from nu-metal to folk rock to Doors and Sex Pistols tribute bands. Music from 7.30pm. (☎224 933 947; www.rockcafe.cz; Národní třída 20; cover free-300Kč; ⏱10am-3am Mon-Fri, 5pm-3am Sat, 5pm-1am Sun; Ⓜ Národní Třída)

Pivovarský Dům (p107)

Shopping

Belda Jewellery JEWELLERY

14 🔒 Map p104, B1

Belda & Co is a long-established Czech firm dating from 1922. Nationalised in 1948, it was revived by the founder's son and grandson, and continues to create gold and silver jewellery of a very high standard. Its range includes its own angular, contemporary designs, as well as reproductions based on art nouveau designs by Alfons Mucha. (☎224 931 052; www.belda.cz; Mikulandská 10; ⏱11am-6pm Mon-Fri; Ⓜ Národní Třída)

Globe Bookstore & Café BOOKS

A popular hang out for book-loving expats, the Globe is a cosy English-language bookshop with an excellent cafe-bar (see **1** ◎ Map 104, B3) in which to peruse your purchases. There's a good range of new fiction and nonfiction, a big selection of secondhand books, and newspapers and magazines in English, French, Spanish, Italian, German and Russian. Also has art exhibitions and film screenings. (☎224 934 203; www.globebookstore.cz; Pštrossova 6; ⏱9.30am-midnight Mon-Thu, to 1am Fri-Sun; 🛜; Ⓜ Karlovo Náměstí)

Local Life
Vyšehrad, Prague's Other Castle

Getting There

Vyšehrad is located high over the banks of the Vltava River, just south of Nové Město.

Ⓜ Line C to Vyšehrad.

🚌 Lines 7, 18, 24 to Ostrčilovo náměstí.

The complex of buildings that make up Vyšehrad Citadel has played an important role in Czech history for more than a thousand years. While not many of the ancient buildings have survived to the present (most structures date from the 18th century, when the complex was used as a fortress), the citadel is still viewed as Prague's spiritual home. For more information and an events calendar, see www.praha-vysehrad.cz.

❶ Through the Old Gates

Heading west, about 10 minutes on foot from the Vyšehrad metro station, you'll pass **Tábor Gate** and the remains of the original Gothic **Špička Gate**.

❷ Prague's Oldest Building

The 11th-century Romanesque **Rotunda of St Martin** is considered Prague's oldest surviving building. The door and frescos date from a renovation made about 1880. It's normally closed, but the interior can be viewed during mass (times posted at the door).

❸ Into the Fortress

Through the **Brick Gate & Casements** (adult/child 50/30Kč; ⊘9.30am-6pm Apr-Oct, to 5pm Nov-Mar) are hidden vaults once used for imprisonment and storing weapons when Vyšehrad served as a fortress in the 18th century. The underground **Gorlice Hall** holds some of the Charles Bridge's original statues.

❹ Outdoor Entertainment

In the warmer months, look out for musical performances and shows at Vyšehrad's open-air theatre, the **Summer Stage** (⊘Apr-Oct).

❺ Dvořák's Final Resting Place

The 600 graves (many with intricately designed headstones) in the lovely gardens of **Vyšehrad Cemetery** (⊘8am-7pm May-Sep, shorter hours Oct-Apr) read like a who's who of Czech arts and letters, including musicians Antonín Dvořák and Bedřich Smetana and artist Alfons Mucha.

❻ Last Church Standing

The neo-Gothic **Church of Sts Peter & Paul** (Kostel sv Petra a Pavla; K Rotundě 10; adult/child 30/10Kč; ⊘9am-noon & 1-5pm Wed-Mon) was one of Vyšehrad's few structures to avoid destruction in 1420 during the Hussite religious wars. The current facade dates from the 19th century.

❼ Dinner While You're Here

Stop for a meal at **Rio's Vyšehrad** (www.riorestaurant.cz; Štulcova 2; mains 250-600Kč; ⊘10am-midnight; 🛜), a classy Mediterranean restaurant featuring excellent fish dishes. Dine on the terrace in nice weather.

❽ Underground History

The atmospheric **Gothic Cellar** (adult/child 50/30Kč; ⊘9.30am-6pm Apr-Oct, to 5pm Nov-Mar) houses a worthwhile exhibit; its overview of the history of Prague's fortification helps put Vyšehrad's sights into perspective.

❾ Beer with a View

Along the fortress's southern ramparts, **Cafe Citadela** (⊘9.30am-6pm) is an outdoor beer garden with a relaxed vibe and nice views. Come for a coffee or beer and enjoy the setting with a young, mostly local crowd.

Explore

Vinohrady & Žižkov

Vinohrady and Žižkov are the yin and yang of residential Prague. Gentrified Vinohrady, named for its days as the royal vineyards, boasts high-ceilinged, art nouveau apartment buildings and is popular with young professionals and expats. The 'people's republic' of Žižkov is historically working class, rebellious and revolutionary, famed for its numerous pubs, alternative nightlife and multicultural population.

PETER FORSBERG/PEOPLE/ALAMY ©

The Sights in a Day

☀ Start your day with a coffee and pastry at one of the cafes around Peace Square (náměstí Míru), the centre of Vinohrady and easily reached by metro. We love **Bio Zahrada** (p121), a short walk from the square. Take the metro one stop to Jiřiho z Poděbrad and admire the modern **Church of the Most Sacred Heart of Our Lord** (p118). From here, it's just a short walk to the **TV Tower** (p118) in Žižkov, where you can ride to the top or simply ogle the larger-than-life baby statues crawling up the outside.

☼ There are lots of good lunch options in the area. Try **The Tavern** (p120) for burgers or down-to-earth Czech fare at **Pastička** (p121). If you get a sunny afternoon, relax at the neighborhood's **Riegrovy sady** (p121) park, where locals congregate for leisurely strolls and beer drinking.

☾ For evenings, try an elegant Italian dinner at **Aromi** (p120) or some tapas at the very popular **Kofein** (p119). Finish the day with some live music at **Palác Akropolis** (p123) or dancing at **Techtle Mechtle** (p123) or **Termix** (p115).

For a local's drinking tour of Vinohrady & Žižkov, see p114.

Q Local Life

Drinking Tour of Vinohrady & Žižkov (p114)

💜 Best of Prague

Cafes & Pubs

Bio Zahrada (p121)

U Slovanské Lípy (p122)

Prague Beer Museum (p115)

Eating

Kofein (p119)

Bisos (p120)

The Tavern (p120)

Nightlife

Palác Akropolis (p123)

Techtle Mechtle (p123)

Radost FX (p123)

Gay & Lesbian

Termix (p115)

Café Celebrity (p122)

Getting There

Metro Line A to Náměstí Míru, Jiřiho z Poděbrad or Flora.

Tram Lines 4, 10, 16, or 22 to Náměstí Míru, line 11 to Jiřiho z Poděbrad.

Local Life
Drinking Tour of Vinohrady & Žižkov

In Prague, there's no better place to make a night of it: Žižkov, on one side, proudly claims to have more pubs per square metre than anywhere else in the world; on the other side, classy Vinohrady is home to some serious wine and cocktail bars, where the staff really know how to mix a drink.

❶ Put Something in Your Stomach

A sturdy meal is always a good idea if a night of drinking is on the cards. **Vinohradský Parlament** (www.vinohrad-skyparlament.cz; Korunní 1; mains 170–239Kč; ⏱11am–midnight Mon–Wed, to 1am Thu–Sat, 11.30am–11.30pm Sun), on Peace Square (náměstí Míru), offers excellent traditional Czech pub food, paired with the best beers offered by the Staropramen brewery.

② **Night at the 'Museum'**

Just across Peace Square, the **Prague Beer Museum** (www.praguebeermuseum. com; Americká 43; ☺noon-3am) – actually a pub – offers 30 regional Czech beers on tap. So, once you've had your fill of Staropramen, see what else the country has to offer.

③ **French Wine with Style**

One metro stop away, at Jiřího z Poděbrad, **Le Caveau** (www.broz-d.cz; náměstí Jiřího z Poděbrad 9; ☺8am-10.30pm Mon-Fri, 9am-10.30pm Sat, 2-8.30pm Sun) offers the city's best selection of French wines and upmarket cheeses and snacks to match. Wine-drinkers may want to start the night right here.

④ **Riegrovy Sady Beer Garden**

A short walk from Jiřího z Poděbrad, the **Riegrovy Sady Beer Garden** (Riegrovy sady; ☺noon-1am May-Sep) is especially popular at night (until around 1am in summer), when the picnic tables fill to bursting with everyone making merry with cheap Gambrinus beer and slightly more expensive Pilsner Urquell.

⑤ **Classy Cocktails at Bar & Books**

At this stage, you can stay classy or go crazy. For classy, **Bar & Books Mánesova** (www.barandbooks.cz; Mánesova 64; ☺5pm-3am) is a sensuous cocktail lounge featuring lush, library-themed decor, top-shelf liquor and live music some nights.

⑥ **Crazy Dancing at Termix**

If crazy is the order of the night and it's after 10pm, gay-friendly **Termix** (www.club-termix.cz; Třebízského 4a; admission free; ☺9pm-5am Wed-Sun) is the place spend the evening. It stays open until 5am or so on weekends, so no need to move on from here if this is your scene.

⑦ **Beer at U Sadu**

For more working-class libations, the congenial neighbourhood pub **U Sadu** (www.usadu.cz; Škroupovo nám 5; ☺8am-4am Tue-Sat, to 2am Sun & Mon) is supremely popular with old locals, dreadlocked students and expats alike. Staff also run the kitchen past midnight here, so if you're craving a snack, this may be your only option.

⑧ **Nightcap at Bukowski's**

On the Žižkov street that's reckoned to have more drinking dens per metre than anywhere else in Prague, **Bukowski's** (Bořivojova 86, Žižkov; ☺7pm-3am), named after the hard-drinking American poet Charles Bukowski, is a cut above its neighbours. Expect cool tunes and confident cocktails.

A   **B**   **C**   **D**

NOVÉ MĚSTO

Náměstí Republiky

Na Florenci

Masarykovo nádraží

National Monument ◉4

Žižkov Hill

Hybernská

Husitská

Senovážné náměstí

Řehořova

Orebitská

Husinecká

Jindřišská

Opletalova

Seifertova

Cimburkova

Miličova

PRAHA 1

U Rajskézahrady

Havelkova

FK Viktoria Žižkov Stadium

Krásova

Víta Nejedlého

Seifertova

Hlavní Nádraží

Wilsonova

Praha hlavní nádraží (Main Train Station)

Vlkova

ŽIŽKOV

Růžová

Vrchlického sady

◎7

16 ✪

Former Jewish Cemetery

Washingtonova

Rajská zahrada

Kubelíkova

Fibichova

TV Tower ◎2

Slavíkova

Křížkovského

Škroupovo náměstí

Mahlerovy sady

Riegrovy sady

Na Švíhance

Chopinova

Krkonošská

Church of the Most Sacred Heart of Our Lord

Muzeum ◎3

Španělská

Helénská

Polská

Polská

Jiřího z Poděbrad

1 ◉

Legerova

Rubešova

Balbínova

Italská

12 ✪

9 ✕

14 ✪

Třebízského

Mánesova

U Kanálky

Jiřího z Poděbrad

náměstí Jiřího z Poděbrad

6 ✕

10 ✕

VINOHRADY

Anny Letenské

17 ✪

Vinohradská

18 ✕

5 ✕

Nitranská

Anglická

Římská

15 ◉

Blanická

Sázavská

Slezská

U Vodárny

Skřétova

19 ✪

Peace Square (náměstí Míru)

Budečská

Šumavská

Korunní

IP Pavlova

Jugoslávská

Náměstí Míru

VINOHRADY

Moravská

Lublaňská

Bělehradská

Rumunská

11 ◉

Belgická

Americká

Varšavská

Francouzská

Lužická

Chodská

Londýnská

Slovenská

Koubkova

Záhřebská

Jana Masaryka

Máchova

Rybalkova

Voroněžská

Kozácká

Donská

Krymská

Wenzigova

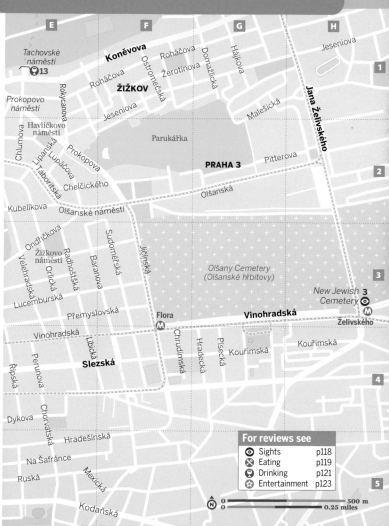

E

F

G

H

Tachovské
náměstí
13

Koněvova

Rohácová

Roháčová

Ostroměšská

Žerotínova

Rohačová

Domažlická

Hájkova

Jeseniova

ŽIŽKOV

Rokycanova

Jeseniova

Jana Želivského

1

Prokopovo
náměstí

Chlumova

Havlíčkovo
náměstí

Lipanská

Lupáčova

Prokopova

Parukářka

Malešická

PRAHA 3

Pitterova

Táboritská

Chelčického

Olšanská

2

Kubelíkova

Olšanské náměstí

Ondříčkova

Žižkovo
náměstí

Radhošťská

Sudoměřská

Jičínská

Olšany Cemetery
(Olšanské hřbitovy)

Velehradská

Orlická

Báranova

New Jewish
Cemetery

3

3

Lucemburská

Přemyslovská

Flora

Vinohradská

Želivského

Vinohradská

Ubická

Slezská

Chrudimská

Hradecká

Písecká

Kouřimská

Kouřimská

Perunova

4

Řipská

Dykova

Chorvatská

Hradešínská

Na Šafránce

Ruská

Mexická

Kodaňská

For reviews see	
⊙ Sights	p118
✕ Eating	p119
☻ Drinking	p121
✿ Entertainment	p123

N 0 ___ 500 m
0 ___ 0.25 miles

5

Sights

Church of the Most Sacred Heart of Our Lord
CHURCH

1 ◎ Map p116, D3

This church, from 1932, is one of Prague's most original pieces of 20th-century architecture. It's the work of Jože Plečnik, a Slovenian architect who also worked on Prague Castle. The church is inspired by Egyptian temples and early Christian basilicas. It's usually only open to the public during mass. (Kostel Nejsvětějšího Srdce Páně; ☎ 222 727 713; www.srdcepane.cz; náměstí Jiřího z Poděbrad 19, Vinohrady; ◷ services 8am & 6pm Mon-Sat, 9am, 11am & 6pm Sun; Ⓜ Jiřího z Poděbrad)

TV Tower
TOWER

2 ◎ Map p116, D3

Prague's tallest landmark – and, depending on your tastes, either its ugliest or its most futuristic feature – is the 216m-tall TV Tower, erected between 1985 and 1992. But more bizarre than its architecture are the 10 giant crawling babies that appear to be exploring the outside of the tower – an installation called **Miminka** (Mummy), by artist David Černý; see p120 for more). (Televizní Vysílač; ☎ 210 320 081; www.towerpark.cz; Mahlerovy sady 1, Žižkov; adult/child/family 180/100/420Kč; ◷ observation decks 8am-midnight; Ⓜ Jiřího z Poděbrad)

New Jewish Cemetery
CEMETERY

3 ◎ Map p116, H3

Franz Kafka is buried in this cemetery, which opened around 1890 when the older Jewish cemetery – now at the foot of the TV Tower – was closed. To find **Kafka's grave**, follow the main avenue east (signposted), turn right at row 21, then left at the wall; it's at the end of the 'block'. Fans make a pilgrimage on 3 June, the anniversary

---

Understand
Not Big in Belgium

Design buffs beware. When Czechs talk about 'Brussels style', they're not referring to Belgian art nouveau or anything related to Henry Van de Velde. Rather, they're harking back to a heyday of their own national design when, despite the constraints of working under a communist regime, Czechoslovakia triumphed with its circular restaurant pavilion at the 1958 Brussels Expo. More than a hundred local designers took away awards, including porcelain designer Jaroslav Ježek, who won the Grand Prix for his Elka coffee service. The aesthetics of the time were similar to what you see at Café Kaaba (p121). For a more authentic take, visit **Veletržní Palác** (☎ 224 301 122; www.ngprague.cz; Dukelských hrdinů 47; adult/concession 200/100Kč; ◷ 10am-6pm Tue-Sun; Ⓜ Vltavská, 🚊 1, 8, 12, 17, 24, 25, 26 to Strossmayerovo náměstí).

JONATHAN SMITH/GETTY IMAGES ©

Miminka (Mummy) sculpture, by David Černý, TV Tower

of his death. (Nový židovské hřbitov; ☎226 235 216; www.kehilaprag.cz; Izraelská 1, Žižkov; admission free; ◷9am-5pm Sun-Thu, to 2pm Fri Apr-Oct, 9am-4pm Sun-Thu, to 2pm Fri Nov-Mar, closed on Jewish holidays; Ⓜ Želivského)

National Monument
MUSEUM

4 ◎ Map p116, D1

While this monument's massive functionalist structure has all the elegance of a nuclear power station, the interior is a spectacular extravaganza of polished art deco marble, gilt and mosaics, and home to a fascinating museum of 20th-century Czechoslovak history. (Národní Památník na Vítkově; ☎222 781 676; www.nm.cz; U Památníku 1900, Žižkov; exhibition only adult/child 60/30Kč, roof

terrace 80/40Kč, combined ticket 110/60Kč; ◷10am-6pm Wed-Sun Apr-Oct, to 6pm Thu-Sun Nov-Mar; ☐133, 175, 207)

Eating

Kofein
SPANISH €€

5 Map p116, D4

One of the hottest restaurants in town is this Spanish-style tapas place not far from the Jiřího z Poděbrad metro station. Descend into a lively space to see a red-faced chef minding the busy grill. Our faves include marinated trout with horseradish and pork belly confit with celeriac. Service is prompt and friendly. Book ahead. (☎273 132 145; www.ikofein.cz; Nitranská 9, Vinohrady; 3

tapas plates 270Kč; ⊘11am-midnight Mon-Fri, 5pm-midnight Sat & Sun; ?◊; 🚌11 , Ⓜ Jiřího z Poděbrad)

Aromi ITALIAN €€€

6 Map p116, D4

Red brick, polished wood and country-style furniture create a rustic atmosphere in this gourmet Italian restaurant. Brisk and businesslike at lunchtime, romantic in the evening, Aromi has a reputation for authentic, excellent Italian cuisine. Advance booking essential. (✆222 713 222; www. aromi.cz; Mánesova 78, Vinohrady; mains 400-600Kč; ⊘noon-11pm Mon-Sat, to 10pm Sun; ?; 🚌11 to Jiřího z Poděbrad, Ⓜ Jiřího z Poděbrad)

Bisos ITALIAN €€

7 Map p116, C2

The lyrics of a love song (in Sardinian dialect) by Sardinian band Tazenda adorn the walls of this cool little restaurant on the fringes of Žižkov.

And you may well fall in love with the food (also Sardinian), ranging from unusual breakfast dishes (buckwheat pancake with goat's cheese, pistachios and maple syrup) to seafood sauté and venison with pumpkin purée. (✆608 550 970; bisos.eu; U Rajské zahrady 16, Žižkov; mains 255-355Kč; ⊘7.30am-11.30pm Tue-Sun; ?; 🚌5, 9, 26)

The Tavern BURGERS €

8 Map p116, C3

This cosy sit-down burger joint is the dream of a husband-and-wife team of American expats who wanted to create the perfect burger using organic products and free-range, grass-fed beef. Great pulled-pork sandwiches, fries and bourbon-based cocktails too. Reservations are taken only over the website or email and only for dinner on Thursday, Friday and Saturday. (www. eng.thetavern.cz; Chopinova 26, Vinohrady; burgers 139-199Kč; ⊘5-10pm Tue, 11.30am-10pm Wed-Sun; 🚌11, Ⓜ Jiřího z Poděbrad)

Understand
How the Tower Got Its Babies

It was Czech artist/provacateur David Černý who first placed the creepy babies on the side of the Žižkov TV Tower in an installation called *Miminka* (Mummy), timed for Prague's reign as European Capital of Culture in 2000. The babies came down at the end of that year, but the resultant public outcry saw them reinstated, and it seems they're now a permanent fixture.

We're no art critics here, but the babies *are* sporting slotted faces, like a USB drive, lending at least one interpretation that the installation is intended as a commentary on our overdependence on media for sustenance. Or maybe not. Come to think of it, the tower *does* look a bit like a baby's bottle...

Pastička
CZECH €€

9 Map p116, B3

A warm, inviting ground-floor pub with a little garden out the back, Pastička is great for a beer or a meal. The interior design is part 1920s Prague and part Irish pub. Most come for the beer, but the mix of international and traditional Czech dishes is very good. (✆222 253 228; www.pasticka. cz; Blanická 25, Vinohrady; mains 149-429Kč; ⏰11am-1am Mon-Fri, 5pm-1am Sat & Sun; 🖥; 🚊11, Ⓜ Jiřího z Poděbrad)

Mozaika
INTERNATIONAL €€

10 Map p116, D4

One of the most dependably good restaurants in the neighbourhood. The theme is an updated French bistro, with beef tournedos and boeuf bourguignon sharing the spotlight with international entrees such as stir-fries, chicken breasts and, our personal favourite (occasionally on the menu): salmon wrapped in seaweed and served with wasabi mashed potatoes. Excellent wine list. Advance booking essential. (✆224 253 011; www. restaurantmozaika.cz; Nitranská 13, Vinohrady; mains 180-450Kč; 🖥; Ⓜ Jiřího z Poděbrad)

Drinking

Bio Zahrada
CAFE

11 Map p116, B5

This organic coffee shop serves high-end coffees and pastries in a

Local Life

Riegrovy Sady

The hilltop park **Riegrovy sady** (Rieger Gardens; entrance on Chopinova, across from Na Švíhance, Vinohrady; ⏰24hr; Ⓜ Jiřího z Poděbrad) gets press for its popular beer garden, but the green space itself is worthy of a visit. On the park's western side, a long grassy slope offers a magnificent view of Prague Castle and the city's red roofs. For a little peace and quiet, grab a beer or a sandwich from the beer garden (p115), or a smaller cafe in the park, and seat yourself on a wooden bench.

welcoming, rustic setting with a big garden out back. It also serves light food items, including a daily, good-value lunch special with veggie curries and risottos for 129Kč. There's a small shop at the front that specialises in organic food items, including pastries, grains, dairy products and tofu. (✆222 518 698; www.bio-zahrada.cz; Belgická 33, Vinohrady; ⏰8.30am-9pm Mon-Thu, to 10pm Fri, 10am-8pm Sat; 🖥; Ⓜ Náměstí Míru)

Café Kaaba
CAFE

12 Map p116, B3

Café Kaaba is a stylish little cafe-bar with retro furniture and pastel-hued decor that comes straight out of the 1959 Ideal Homes Exhibition. It serves up excellent coffee (made with freshly ground imported beans). Note that the wi-fi is only free for customers from opening until 6pm.

Nonsmoking until 9pm. (☎222 254 021; www.kaaba.cz; Mánesova 20, Vinohrady; ⏰8am-11pm Mon-Fri, 9am-11pm Sat, 10am-11pm Sun; 🛜; 🚋11)

U Slovanské Lípy PUB

13 Map p116, E1

A classic Žižkov pub, plain and unassuming outside and in, 'At the Linden Trees' (the linden is a Czech and Slovak national emblem) is something of a place of pilgrimage for beer lovers. The reason is its range of artisan brews, such as those from the Kout na Šumavě brewery, including a superb *světlý ležák* (pale lager). (☎734 743 094; www. uslovanskelipy.cz; Tachovské náměstí 6, Žižkov; ⏰11am-midnight; 🛜♿; 🚋133, 175, 207)

Saints BAR

14 Map p116, C3

Sealing the deal on Prague's booming 'gay quarter' in Vinohrady, this British-run bar is laid-back, friendly and serves good drinks. With a multinational staff speaking many languages, for newcomers it's the perfect starter to the local scene. (☎222 250 326; www.saintsbar.cz; Polská 32, Vinohrady; ⏰7pm-2am Sun-Thu, to 4am Fri & Sat; Ⓜ Jiřího z Poděbrad)

Café Celebrity CAFE

15 Map p116, B4

This cafe is part of the cluster of gay-friendly places that make up the old Radio Palác building. The Celebrity offers early-morning breakfasts on weekdays and a more relaxed brunch on weekends. At other times, it's great for coffee and people-watching. (☎222 511 343; www.celebritycafe.cz; Vinohradská 40, Vinohrady; ⏰8am-2am Mon-Fri, 10am-2am Sat, 10am-midnight Sun; 🛜; Ⓜ Náměstí Míru)

Understand
Absinth(e) Makes the Heart Grow Fonder

For many visitors, Prague is synonymous with absinth. That's been the case since the 1990s, when Czech drinks firm Hills cleverly revived this long-banned, legendary and allegedly hallucinatory 19th-century French-Swiss tipple. Today, however, the Swiss and French have resumed production of the genuine 'green fairy', and true connoisseurs hold their noses when it comes to replica 'Czechsinths'.

What's the difference? Most Czech brands (whether spelt absinth or absinthe) use oil to mix the active ingredient, wormwood, into the liquid, instead of properly distilling it. If you'll be packing a bottle in your suitcase, try the pricey but excellent Czech-made absinth Toulouse Lautrec (about 1200Kč at shops around town).

Entertainment

Palác Akropolis
LIVE MUSIC

16 Map p116, D2

The Akropolis is a Prague institution, a smoky, labyrinthine, sticky-floored shrine to alternative music and drama. Its various performance spaces host a smorgasbord of musical and cultural events, from DJs to string quartets to Macedonian Roma bands to local rock gods to visiting talent – Marianne Faithfull, the Flaming Lips and the Strokes have all played here. (📞296 330 911; www.palacakropolis. cz; Kubelíkova 27, Žižkov; cover free-200Kč; 🕙club 7pm-5am; 🛜; 🚋5, 9, 26 to Lipanska)

Techtle Mechtle
DANCE

17 Map p116, B4

A popular cellar dance bar on Vinohrady's main drag. The name translates to 'hanky panky' in Czech and that's what most of the swanky people who come here are after. In addition to a well-tended cocktail bar, you'll find a decent restaurant and dance floor, and occasional special events. Arrive early to get a good table. (📞222 250 143; www.techtle-mechtle. cz; Vinohradská 47, Vinohrady; 🕙6pm-4am Tue-Thu, to 5am Fri & Sat; 🛜; Ⓜ Náměstí Míru, 🚋11 to Vinohradská tržnice)

Termix
DANCE

18 Map p116, C4

Termix is one of Prague's most popular gay dance clubs, with an industrial hi-tech vibe (lots of shiny steel, glass and plush sofas) and a young crowd that contains as many tourists as locals. The smallish dance floor fills up fast and you may have to queue to get in. (📞222 710 462; www.club-termix. cz; Třebízského 4a, Vinohrady; admission free; 🕙9pm-5am Wed-Sun; Ⓜ Jiřího z Poděbrad)

Radost FX
DANCE

19 Map p116, A4

Though not quite as trendy as it once was, slick and shiny Radost is still capable of pulling in the crowds, with themed dance parties each night of the week. The regular Thursday night hip-hop and R & B party remains the most popular. The place has a chilled-out, bohemian atmosphere, with an excellent lounge and vegetarian restaurant. (📞224 254 776; www.radostfx.cz; Bělehradská 120, Vinohrady; cover 100-250Kč; 🕙10pm-6am; 🛜; Ⓜ IP Pavlova)

Explore

Holešovice

In Holešovice, you start to appreciate Prague as a genuine work-ing city. Though sections of this former industrial quarter remain somewhat rundown, the neighbourhood has been slowly gentrifying. The hilltop beer garden at Letná is a relaxing spot on a warm even-ing in summer, while the National Gallery's impressive holdings at Veletržní Palác may be Prague's most underrated museum.

The Sights in a Day

 Start the morning with culture. If you're travelling with kids, head for the **National Technical Museum** (p129), with its giant hall filled with historic locomotives and antique cars. If you're on your own, go for the eye-opening collection of modern art at the **Veletržní Palác** (p126). There are a lot of good cafes in the neighbourhood for a pick-me-up drink or some lunch – we like **Kumbal** (p131), just a short walk from the Veletržní Palác.

After lunch, get some fresh air at one of the neighbourhood's two big parks: **Letná Gardens** (p129) or **Stromovka** (p129). The former has a handy beer garden, where an afternoon can easily slide into evening. Stromovka has more room to roam and is close to **Zoo Mořský Svět** (p129), the city's largest aquarium and another good spot for kids.

Holešovice is short on good restaurants, but **Fraktal** (p131) has a killer burger and the Italian food at **Peperoncino** (p130) is good value. Both are close to Letná Gardens. In the mood for a show? **Křižík's Fountain** (p129) pairs water gyrations with classical music. For clubbing, there's funky, postindustrial **Cross Club** (p132) or upscale **Mecca** (p132).

👁 Top Sights

Veletržní Palác (p126)

❤ Best of Prague

Bars & Pubs

Letná Beer Garden (p130)

Fraktal (p131)

Museums

Veletržní Palác (p126)

National Technical Museum (p129)

DOX Centre for Contemporary Art (p132)

For Kids

Stromovka (p129)

Zoo Mořský Svět (p129)

Nightlife

Cross Club (p132)

Mecca (p132)

SaSaZu (p132)

Getting There

🚋 **Tram** Lines 1, 8, 12, 25, 26 to Letenské náměstí; lines 1, 5, 8, 12, 17, 24, 25, 26 to Strossmayerovo náměstí.

Ⓜ **Metro** Line C to Vltavská or Nádraží Holešovice.

Top Sights
Veletržní Palác

The National Gallery's collection of art from the 19th, 20th and 21st centuries is a must for serious art lovers, particularly fans of those modern movements – such as impressionism, constructivism, Dadaism and surrealism – that shattered the art world in the early 20th century. The holdings are strong on French impressionists, early modern masters like Schiele, Klimt and Picasso, and the talented generation of Czech artists working in the 1920s and '30s. Side exhibits look at trends in architecture and design.

Map p128, C3

www.ngprague.cz

Dukelských hrdinů 47

adult/concession 200/100Kč

10am-6pm Tue-Sun

1, 8, 12, 17, 24, 25, 26 to Strossmayerovo náměstí

National Gallery, Veletržní Palác

Don't Miss

French Collection

Thanks to a strong Bohemian interest in French painting, the palace's 3rd floor has an impressive collection of 19th- and 20th-century French art. Artists represented include Monet, Gauguin, Cézanne, Picasso, Delacroix and Rodin. Look for Gauguin's *Flight* and Van Gogh's *Green Wheat*.

Avant-Garde Czech Art

The museum's display of 20th-century Czech art (also on the 3rd floor) is one of the country's finest. Standouts include the geometric works by František Kupka, and cubist paintings, ceramics and design by several different artists – these paintings show an interesting parallel with the concurrent art scene in Paris. On the 2nd floor, look for the most contemporary Czech works across several genres.

Female Imagery in the International Collection

The 20th-century international collection, on the 1st floor, boasts works by some major names: Klimt, Schiele, Sherman and Miró, to name a few. Two highlights take on feminine themes: Klimt's luscious, vibrantly hued *The Virgins* and Schiele's much darker, foreboding *Pregnant Woman and Death*.

Alfons Mucha's *Slav Epic*

Through 2015 at least, the museum is also exhibiting Alfons Mucha's grandiose *Slav Epic (Slovanská epopej)*, a collection of 20 giant paintings that tell the story of the Slavic peoples. Mucha dedicated much of his career to creating these canvasses. Entry requires a separate admission ticket.

☑ Top Tips

▶ The museum is huge. If you only have an hour or two, just hit the highlights listed here.

▶ If you're travelling with children, the museum offers a family pass for the discounted price of 250Kč.

▶ Pick up Prague postcards or souvenirs at the museum shop.

✕ Take a Break

The museum cafe, located on the ground floor and open during museum hours, is convenient for a coffee.

A few blocks away, the funky cafe Kumbal (p131) is a charming place for coffee or lunch.

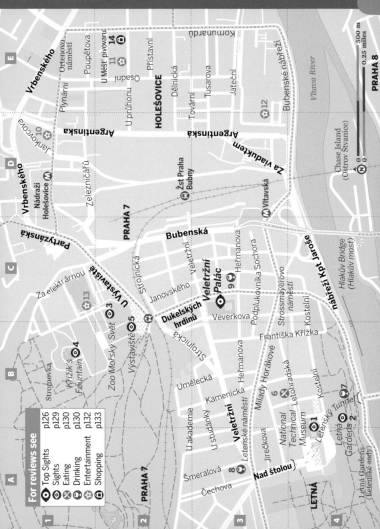

PRAHA 8

Vltava River

Chase Island
(Ostrov Štvanice)

0   500 m
0   0.25 miles

Hlávkův Bridge
(Hlávkův most)

nábřeží Kpt Jaroše

Kostelní

Letohradská

Letná
Gardens

Letenský Tunnel

Letná Gardens
(Letenské sady)

LETNÁ

National
Technical
Museum

Milady Horákové

Strossmayerovo
náměstí

Podplukovníka Sochora

Hermanova

Veletržní
Palác

Bubenská

Heřmanova

Za viaduktem

Argentinská

HOLEŠOVICE

Bubenské nábřeží

Komunardů

Přístavní

Poupětova

Ortenovo
náměstí

U Měšť pivovaru

Osadní

Dělnická

Tovární

Tusarova

Jateční

U průhonu

Argentinská

Žst Praha
Bubny

Vltavská

Železničářů

Nádraží
Holešovice

Jankovcova

Pynárni

Vrbenského

Vrbenského

Partyzánská

Za elektrárnou

Strojnická

U Výstaviště

Křížik's
Fountain

Zoo Mořský Svět

Výstaviště

Stromovka

Janovského

Veletržní

Dukelských
hrdinů

Veverkova

Františka Křížka

Veletržní

Kamenická

Umělecká

U akademie

U studánky

Letenské náměstí

Jirečkova

Šmeralová

Čechova

Nad štolou

PRAHA 7

PRAHA 7

For reviews see
- ◆ Top Sights   p126
- ◉ Sights   p129
- ⊗ Eating   p130
- ❸ Drinking   p130
- ✪ Entertainment   p132
- ⊜ Shopping   p133

◆ Veletržní Palác **9**

◉ **3** ◉ **5** ◉ **4**

✪ **13** ✪ **12**

◉ **1** ◉ **2**

6

7

8

10

11 **14**

E D C B A

1 2 3 4

N

Sights

National Technical Museum
MUSEUM

1 ⊙ Map p128, B4

Prague's most family-friendly museum got a high-tech renovation in 2012 and is a dazzling presentation of the country's industrial heritage. If that sounds dull, it's anything but. Start in the main hall, filled to the rafters with historic planes, trains and automobiles. There are separate halls devoted to exhibits on astronomy, photography, printing and architecture. (Národní Technické Muzeum; ☎220 399 111; www.ntm.cz; Kostelní 42; adult/concession 190/90Kč; ⊙9am-5.30pm Tue-Fri, 10am-6pm Sat & Sun; ⚹; ◻1, 8, 12, 25, 26 to Letenské náměstí)

Letná Gardens
PARK

2 ⊙ Map p128, B4

Lovely Letná Gardens is a large park that occupies a bluff over the Vltava river, north of the Old Town, with postcard-perfect views out over the city, river and bridges. It's ideal for walking, jogging and beer drinking at a popular beer garden (p130) at the eastern end. The entrance is 10 minutes on foot south of Letenské náměstí. (Letenské sady; ⊙24hr; ⚹; ◻1, 8, 12, 25, 26 to Letenské náměstí)

Zoo Mořský Svět
AQUARIUM

3 ⊙ Map p128, C2

The Czech 'Sea World' has the largest water tank in the country, with a capacity of around 100,000L. Some 4500 living species of fish and sea creatures are on display, with a good (and suitably scary) set of sharks. The cramped interior will be disappointing if you're used to larger 'Sea World'–type amusement parks around the world. (☎220 103 275; www.morskysvet.cz; U Výstaviště 1, Bubeneč; adult/concession 280/180Kč; ⊙10am-7pm; ⚹; ◻12, 17, 24 to Výstaviště)

Křižík's Fountain
FOUNTAIN

4 ⊙ Map p128, B1

Each evening from spring to autumn the musical Křižík's Fountain performs its computer-controlled light-and-water dance. Performances range

Local Life
Stromovka Park

Prague's largest central park, **Stromovka** (Královská obora; entry at Výstaviště or Nad Královskou oborou 21, Bubeneč; ◻1, 8, 12, 25, 26 to Letenské náměstí), was once a medieval hunting ground for royals; now it's popular with strollers, joggers, cyclists and in-line skaters. Kids can climb on the huge gnarled branches of ancient fallen trees or play at one of several playgrounds – and adults will appreciate the lavish tulip display in spring.

from classical music such as Dvořák's *New World Symphony* to rousing works performed by Andrea Bocelli, Queen or Scorpions. Check the website for what's on. The show is best after sunset – from May to July go for later shows. (Křižíkova fontána; ☑723 665 694; www.krizikovafontana.cz; U Výstaviště 1, Bubeneč; admission 220Kč; ☺performances hourly 8-11pm Mar-Oct; 👬; 🚊12, 17, 24 to Výstaviště)

Výstaviště
PUBLIC SPACE

 5 Map p128, B2

A sprawling area of attractions and buildings of various architectural styles that was first laid out for the 1891 Jubilee Exhibition. These days it holds mainly trade fairs, but also has a branch of the **National Museum**

Local Life
Prague Zoo

Prague's attractive **zoo** (Zoo Praha; ☑296 112 230; www.zoopraha.cz; U Trojského zámku 120, Troja; adult/ concession/family 200/150/600Kč; ☺9am-7pm Jun-Aug, to 6pm Apr, May, Sep & Oct, to 5pm Mar, to 4pm Nov-Feb; 👬; 🚊112, M Nádraží Holešovice) is set in 60 hectares of wooded grounds on the banks of the Vltava. It makes for a great outing for kids. There are sizeable collections of giraffes and gorillas, but pride of place goes to a herd of rare horses. Attractions include a miniature cable car and a big play area.

(☑233 375 636; www.nm.cz; U Výstaviště 1, Bubeneč; adult/concession 50/30Kč; ☺noon-6pm Wed-Sun Apr-Oct; 🚊12, 17, 24 to Výstaviště), a 'singing fountain' (p129), the city's biggest aquarium (p129) and a slightly scruffy amusement park that's open daily from April to October. (Exhibition Grounds; ☑220 103 111; www.incheba.cz; Areál Výstaviště, Bubeneč; ☺9am-11pm; 🚊12, 17, 24 to Výstaviště)

Eating

Peperoncino
ITALIAN €€

6 Map p128, B3

Insider's choice for good, reasonably priced Italian cooking in the western end of Holešovice. The grilled octopus and beans starter is a neighbourhood favourite, but we're partial to the beef or tuna carpaccio. The pastas and main courses are all excellent, and the wine list has lots of affordable Czech and Italian choices. Beautiful, bucolic garden in summer. Reservations recommended. (☑233 312 438; www.restaurant-peperoncino.cz; Letohradská 34; mains 180-390Kč; ☺11am-11pm; 🗲; 🚊1, 8, 12, 25, 26 to Letenské náměstí)

Drinking

Letná Beer Garden
BEER GARDEN

 7 Map p128, B4

No accounting of watering holes in the neighbourhood would be complete without a nod towards the city's best

RICHARD NEBESKY/GETTY IMAGES ©

Letná Beer Garden

beer garden, situated at the eastern end of the Letná Gardens (p129). Buy a takeaway beer from a small kiosk and grab a picnic table, or sit on a small terrace where you can order beer by the glass and decent pizza. (☑233 378 208; www.letenskyzamecek.cz; Letenské sady 341; ☺11am-11pm summer only; ☐1, 8, 12, 25, 26 to Letenské náměstí)

Fraktal   BAR

8 ☺ Map p128, A3

This subterranean space under a corner house near Letenské náměstí is easily the friendliest bar this side of the Vltava. This is especially true for English-speakers, as Fraktal serves as a kind of unofficial expat watering hole. There's also good bar fare such as burgers. The only drawback is the early closing time (last orders at 11.30pm). (☑777 794 094; www.fraktalbar. cz; Šmeralová 1, Bubeneč; mains 120-300Kč; ☺; ☐1, 8, 12, 25, 26 to Letenské náměstí)

Kumbal   CAFE

9 ☺ Map p128, C3

This stylish coffee bar in a 1930s functionalist building manages to be both hip and comfortable at the same time. There are good coffee and tea drinks, though not much on the menu aside from a few simple sandwiches and a daily soup (usually vegetarian).

Breakfast is served every day until 11.30am. (📞604 959 323; www.kumbal.cz; Heřmanová 12; ⏰8am-9.30pm Mon-Fri, 9am-9.30pm Sat & Sun; 🛜🎫; 🚊1, 8, 12, 17, 24, 25, 26 to Strossmayerovo náměstí)

Entertainment

Cross Club
DJ, LIVE MUSIC

10 ⭐ Map p128, D1

An industrial club in every sense of the word: the setting in an industrial zone; the thumping music (both DJs and live acts); and the interior, an absolute must-see jumble of gadgets,

shafts, cranks and pipes, many of which move and pulsate with light to the music. The program includes occasional live music, theatre performances and art happenings. (📞736 535 010; www.crossclub.cz; Plynární 23; cover free-150Kč; ⏰cafe noon-2am, club 6pm-4am; 🛜; Ⓜ Nádraží Holešovice)

Mecca
DJ

11 ⭐ Map p128, E2

This former warehouse in Holešovice had a slick renovation and now boasts fun on three floors (and five bars). It's weekends only, with Friday usually given over to a weekly R&B party featuring DJs from around the country and occasionally around Europe. The crowd tends to be a bit older – professionals in their 20s, 30s and 40s. (📞734 155 300; www.mecca.cz; U Průhonu 3; cover 100-200Kč; ⏰10pm-6am Fri & Sat; 🛜; 🚊1, 12, 14, 25)

SaSaZu
DJ, DANCE

12 ⭐ Map p128, D3

One of the most popular dance clubs in the city, Sasazu attracts the fashionable elite and hangers-on in equal measure. If you're into big dance floors and long lines (hint: go early), this is your place. Check the website for occasional big-name acts (such as Bastille or Morcheeba). Book a table in advance by phone (10am to 6pm Monday to Friday, 4pm to 10pm Saturday). (📞778 054 054; www.sasazu.com; Bubenské nábřeží 306, Hall 25, Pražská Tržnice; admission 200-1000Kč; ⏰9pm-5am; 🛜; 🚊1, 14, 25 to Pražská Tržnice, Ⓜ Vltavská)

🔍 Local Life
DOX Centre for Contemporary Art

Just a short tram ride away from Veletržní Palác, the **DOX Centre for Contemporary Art** (📞295 568 123; www.dox.cz; Poupětova 1; adult/concession 180/90Kč; ⏰10am-6pm Mon, 11am-7pm Wed & Fri, 11am-9pm Thu, 10am-6pm Sat & Sun; 🚊12, 14, 24 to Ortenovo náměstí) is a private gallery and museum that's trying to re-establish Holešovice's reputation as repository of Prague's best modern art. This minimalist multi-level building occupies an entire corner block, providing Prague's most capacious gallery space, studded with a diverse range of thought-provoking contemporary art and photography. Don't miss DOX's excellent cafe and bookshop.

Mecca

Tipsport Aréna
SPECTATOR SPORT

13 ⭐ Map p128, C1

You can see the ice-hockey team HC Sparta Praha – Czech Extraliga champions in 2006 and 2007 – play at the 13,000-capacity Tipsport Aréna beside the exhibition grounds in Holešovice. Buy tickets online at www.ticketportal. cz or at the stadium box office before matches. (Sportovní Hala; ☎266 727 443; http://tipsportarena-praha.cz; Za elektrárnou 419; match tickets 180-400Kč; ☉box office 1-5.30pm Mon-Fri; ☒12, 17, 24 to Výstaviště, Ⓜ Nádraží Holešovice)

Shopping

Pivní Galerie
FOOD, DRINK

14 🔒 Map p128, E2

If you think Czech beer begins and ends with Pilsner Urquell, a visit to the tasting room at Pivní Galerie (the Beer Gallery) will lift the scales from your eyes. Here you can sample and purchase a huge range of Bohemian and Moravian beers – nearly 150 varieties from 30 different breweries – with expert advice from the owners. (☎220 870 613; www.pivnigalerie.cz; U Průhonu 9; ☉11am-7pm Wed-Fri; ☒1, 12, 14, 25 to U Průhonu)

The Best of
Prague

Old Town Square (p74)
FRANCESCO IACOBELLI/GETTY IMAGES ©

Best Walks
Kafka's Prague

🏃 The Walk

'This narrow circle encompasses my entire life', Franz Kafka (1883–1924) once said, drawing an outline around Prague's Old Town. While an exaggeration (he travelled and died abroad), Prague is a constant, unspoken presence in Kafka's writing, and this walk through the Old Town passes some of his regular haunts.

Start Náměstí Republiky; Ⓜ Náměstí Republiky

Finish Hotel Intercontinental; Ⓜ Staroměstská

Length 2km; 40 minutes

🍴 Take a Break

Near the Spanish Synagogue in Prague's old Jewish neighbourhood, Bakeshop Praha (p65) is a perfect corner spot for gourmet coffee and pastries.

Kafka's birthplace, Old Town Square

JONATHAN SMITH/GETTY IMAGES ©

❶ Worker's Accident Insurance Company

Kafka's fiction was informed by his mundane day job as an insurance clerk; he worked for 14 years (1908–22) at the **Worker's Accident Insurance Company** at Na Poříčí 7. His walk home passed the **Powder Gate** (p79) and the newly built **Municipal House** (p96).

❷ House of the Three Kings

Just before the Old Town Square at Celetná 3 is the **House of the Three Kings**, where the Kafkas lived from 1896 to 1907. Franz's room, overlooking the **Church of Our Lady Before Týn** (p75), is where he wrote his first story.

❸ Sixt House

Across Celetná, the **Sixt House** was an earlier childhood home (1888–89). Nearby, at Staroměstské náměstí 17, is **At the Unicorn** (U Jednorožce) – home to Berta Fanta, who hosted literary salons for thinkers of the day, including Kafka and a young Albert Einstein.

❹ House of the Minute

The **House of the Minute** (dům U minuty), the Renaissance corner building attached to the Old Town Hall, was where Franz lived as a young boy (1889–96). He later recalled being dragged to his school in Masná street by the family cook.

❺ Kafka's Birthplace

Just west of the **Church of St Nicholas** (p75) is **Kafka's birthplace**, marked by a bust of him at náměstí Franze Kafky 3. All that remains of the original house is the stone portal.

❻ Kafka's Bachelor Pad

Despite several fraught love affairs, Kafka never married and lived mostly with his parents. One of his few **bachelor flats** can be found at Dlouhá 16.

❼ Bílkova Apartment

Continuing north past the **Franz Kafka monument** (p65) you'll come to another of Kafka's temporary **apartments** at Bílkova 22. In 1914 he began *The Trial* here.

❽ Hotel Intercontinental

Head west to Pařížská and north towards the river. In the **Hotel Intercontinental's grounds** once stood another Kafka family apartment (1907–13), where Franz wrote his Oedipal short story 'The Judgment' (1912), and began *Metamorphosis,* about a man who transformed into a giant insect.

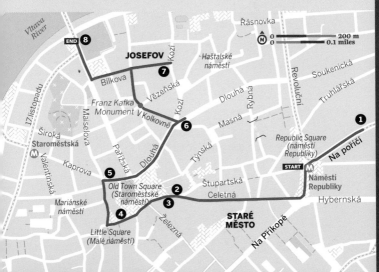

Best Walks
Velvet Revolution

🏃 The Walk

It's been a quarter-century since 1989's Velvet Revolution – when Czechs peacefully overthrew their communist overlords – but it will always be a landmark event. This walk takes you past the sites of the large-scale protests, strikes and press conferences that heralded epic change in the Czech Republic.

Start Národní třída; **M** Národní třída

Finish Former Radio Free Europe Building; **M** Muzeum

Length 2km; 45 minutes

🍴 Take a Break

Found just off Wenceslas Square in a faded but formerly glamorous shopping gallery, Kavárna Lucerna (p93) is an atmospheric place for coffee or a beer.

Jan Palach Memorial (p93)

❶ Student Memorial

We start where the revolution itself began. The **bronze sculpture** under the arches marks the tragic events of 17 November 1989, when tens of thousands of students marching to remember Czechs murdered in WWII were attacked by riot police.

❷ Adria Palace

The beautiful, rondo-cubist **Adria Palace** (Národní třída 36) temporarily served as the headquarters of Civic Forum, the umbrella group formed by Václav Havel to represent the protesters and their demands. In the weeks after 17 November, this was a beehive of dissident activity.

❸ Museum of Communism

The **Museum of Communism** (p96) illuminates local communist history – and the lies, privations and humiliations that ultimately drove the revolution demanding the regime's end. A short, graphic film shows the events of 1989.

4 Melantrich Building

The action soon spread to nearby **Wenceslas Square** (p92) and the **Melantrich Building**. On 24 November, Havel deposed 'Prague Spring' president Alexander Dubček and addressed crowds from its balcony.

5 St Wenceslas Statue

The **Wenceslas Statue** (p93), at the upper end of the square, was bedecked by protesters with flags, posters and political slogans.

6 Činoherní Klub Theatre

Prague's theatres were used for public discussions. The Civic Forum was formed on 19 November at **Činoherní Klub Theatre** (Ve Smečkách 26) and immediately demanded the resignations of communist functionaries.

7 Jan Palach Memorial

Just in front of the **National Museum** (p95) is the **Jan Palach Memorial** (p93), an inlaid cross for a student who set himself on fire in 1969 to protest the Soviet-led Warsaw Pact invasion of the previous year – becoming a national hero in the process.

8 Former Radio Free Europe Building

At the top of the square, left of the National Museum, stands the former building for **Radio Free Europe** (p93), the US-funded radio station that helped bring down the communist regime. It now houses a branch of the National Museum.

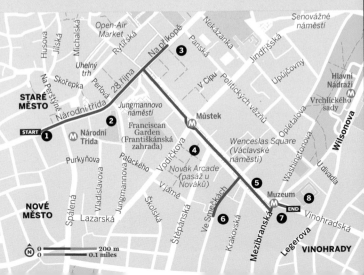

Best Walks
Prague River Walk

🏃 The Walk

The Vltava River runs through the heart of Prague and served as muse for composer Bedřich Smetana in writing his moving 'Vltava' (Moldau) symphony, probably the best-known Czech work of classical music. But you don't need to be a musician to enjoy the river's breathtaking bridges and backdrops on this extended walk along (and across) the waterway.

Start Convent of St Agnes; Ⓜ Staroměstská

Finish Dancing Building; Ⓜ Karlovo Náměstí

Length 8km; three hours

🍴 Take a Break

Perched on the river's edge, old-fashioned Kavárna Slavia (p106) is the place to stop for coffee and cake (though not necessarily a meal). Try for a table by the big windows facing Prague Castle.

SYLVAIN SONNET/GETTY IMAGES ©

Vltava River and Charles Bridge (p76)

❶ Convent of St Agnes

Start the walk outside the **Convent of St Agnes** (p65), the oldest Gothic building in Bohemia – building began in 1231. It's named after Princess Agnes, humanitarian and founder of the only Czech religious order in the 13th century. It's supposedly haunted by the ghost of a nun who was killed by her own father after falling in love with a young man.

❷ Letná Gardens

Crossing Čech Bridge (Čechův most), look out over the river and take in the sun-dappled sights of the castle complex and Petřín Hill. Climb the steps up to the **Metronome** and to **Letná Gardens** (p129). Amble around up here as you like and take in the view of the Old Town and Malá Strana below.

❸ Prague Castle

After you're done gawking, follow the ridge westward (in the direction of castle) for more dramatic views. The path will take you into the interior of the park and across a small bridge all the way to **Prague Castle** (p24). Enjoy the breeze – and more sweeping views over the Vltava and the red roofs of Malá Strana – from the ramparts or from a park bench in the beautifully manicured royal gardens built up along the hillside.

❹ Charles Bridge

From the castle, meander downhill towards another of Prague's chief attractions: the bustling and always gorgeous **Charles Bridge** (p76). Midway across the bridge, find a quiet spot to admire your surroundings – the towering medieval gates, the castle, the lazy river, the skyline of Malá Strana, the green slope of Petřín Hill.

❺ Slav Island

Once on the Old Town side of the river, turn right (south), with another stretch of beautiful photo-op views. To get closer to the water's edge, step onto **Slav Island** (p105). When the weather's warm, you can rent a paddle boat from the stand at one end. Any time of year, it's a delightfully quiet place to enjoy a picnic or take a nap in the shade.

❻ Dancing Building

Heading further south, continue along the river's edge until you reach the whimsical yet elegant **Dancing Building** (p105).

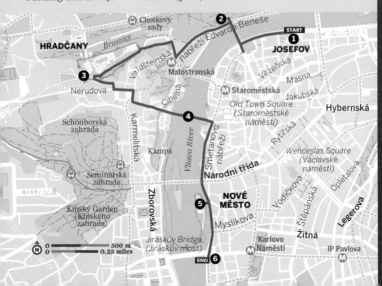

Best
Bars & Pubs

INDOLF POMPE GETTY IMAGES ©

In the Czech Republic, drinking is a national pastime. It's no surprise, then, that Prague is an imbiber's playground. On practically every corner, there's another pub, wine bar, beer hall or cocktail lounge. Though it's traditionally a beer-drinker's city, the landscape is changing – a growing interest in national and international wines plus a trend towards classic cocktails are diversifying the scene.

Beer Basics

When it comes to *pivo* (beer), Czechs prefer *světlé* (light lagers) to *tmavé* (darker beers), though most pubs serve both. Pilsner Urquell is considered the best Czech brand, though Gambrinus, Budvar and Prague's own Staropramen are all popular. Czech beers are usually labelled either *dvanáctka* (12°) or *desítka* (10°) – but this doesn't refer to alcohol content (most beers are 4.5% to 5%). The 12° beers, like Pilsner Urquell, tend to be slightly heavier and stronger than 10° beers.

Microbrews & 'Tank' Beer

The global craft-beer trend has reached the Czech Republic and is most pronounced in Prague, which boasts around a dozen brew pubs where DIY brewers proffer their own concoctions, usually accompanied by good traditional Czech cooking. To compete with the microbrews, the larger breweries have come up with several innovations, including offering *nefiltrované* (unfiltered) beer and hauling beer directly to pubs in supersized tanks (called, unsurprisingly, *tankové pivo*). Tank beer is said to be fresher than beer in traditional kegs, and that sounds good to us.

☑ Top Tips

▶ Pub tabs are usually recorded on a slip of paper on your table; don't write on it or lose it.

▶ You can usually order a beer in a pub without saying anything; when the waiter approaches, just raise your thumb for one beer, or thumb and index finger for two, etc.

▶ To pay up and go, say *zaplatím* (I'll pay).

▶ It's normal to tip a few crowns.

Best for Beer

Prague Beer Museum
Not a museum but a hugely popular pub,

Outdoor restaurant overlooking Vltava River

CHRISTER FREDRIKSSON/GETTY IMAGES ©

with 30 varieties on tap. (p69)

Jáma Rotating selection of regional beers and microbrews. (p99)

U Zlatého Tygra The classic Prague drinking den, where Václav Havel took Bill Clinton in 1994 to show him a real Czech pub. (p84)

Pivovarský Dům Popular microbrewery with several beers on tap and decent Czech food. (p107)

Letná Beer Garden A big beer garden with stunning views over Prague. (p130)

Best Cocktail Bars

Hemingway Bar Snug and sophisticated hideaway. (p84)

Hoffa Popular new bar, completely smoke free. (p99)

Bukowski's Dark and smoky expat cocktail dive. (p115)

Čili Bar Cute and compact, serves rum with chopped chilli peppers. (p84)

Tretter's New York Bar Upmarket New York–style cocktail bar. (p67)

Best for Wine

Bokovka Extensive menu of top-notch Moravian wines. (p108)

Le Caveau Cosy Vinohrady watering hole and deli features excellent French wine. (p115)

Café Kaaba Retro cafe that stocks wines from around the world

and sells by the glass. (p121)

Best Cafes

Grand Cafe Orient A stunning cubist gem with a sunny balcony. (p84)

Cafe Louvre Prague's most agreeable grand cafe and billiards hall. (p106)

Kavárna Obecní dům A legendary Viennese-style coffee house inside the art nouveau landmark. (p84)

Café Savoy This gorgeous coffee house does a lavish breakfast. (p50)

Krásný ztráty Student cafe that doubles as an art gallery and occasional music venue. (p84)

Best
Food

The restaurant scene in Prague gets better with each passing year. The latest trend is 'slow food' – traditional dishes given a refresh with locally sourced ingredients and less fat and starch. Recent years have seen an explosion in vegetarian and vegan restaurants, and international trends are strong as well.

YADID LEVY/GETTY IMAGES ©

Czech Cuisine

Czech food in Prague can be hit-and-miss. Traditional dishes like *vepřová pečeně s knedlíky* (roast pork and sliced bread dumplings) or *svíčková na smetaně* (roast beef in cream sauce) can be bland (as at many touristy restaurants in the centre) or memorable (when prepared by someone who cares). Other, often delicious, Czech staples include *vepřové koleno* (pork knuckle), *kachna* (duck) and *guláš* (goulash), served with beef or pork and bread dumplings.

International Foods

Alongside standard international cuisines like French and Italian (and especially pizza), Czechs have developed a taste for good Indian and Asian cooking as well as for steakhouses and Mexican food. The latest trends at time of writing include steakhouses, gourmet burgers and Vietnamese restaurants.

Vegetarian Options

The past few years has witnessed a revolution in healthy dining, with a growing number of vegetarian and vegan restaurants sprouting up around town. Vegetarian options at traditional Czech restaurants seem to be limited, with the best bet being the ubiquitous *smažený sýr* (fried cheese), served with a dollop of cranberry and/or tartar sauce.

☑ **Top Tips**

▸ Some places charge a small *couvert* (to cover bread and condiments); this should be clearly marked on the menu.

▸ A 10% tip is customary but check to see it hasn't already been added to the bill.

▸ Avoid restaurants directly on Old Town Square and in the most heavily touristed zones – these are invariably mediocre.

Bakeshop Praha (p65)

Best Fine Dining

V zátiší From high-end Indian cuisine to gourmet versions of traditional Czech dishes. (p82)

Kalina A little touch of Gallic sophistication in Staré Město. (p81)

Chagall's Understated style, French flair and a warm welcome. (p66)

Best Czech Cuisine

Lokál Classic Czech dishes and great beer in a bright, modern beer hall. (p66)

Kolkovna A stylish, modern take on the traditional Prague pub. (p66)

Elegantes Ultra-high-end Czech food served in a sophisticated setting. (p50)

Best for Vegetarians

Country Life Prague's first-ever health-food shop is an all-vegan cafeteria. (p82)

Lehká Hlava Exotic dining room with an emphasis on fresh preparation. (p82)

Maitrea Quality vegetarian and vegan cuisine

amid unexpected designer decor. (p82)

Best for a Quick Lunch

Globe Bookstore & Café Varied range of international classics plus an excellent brunch menu. (p105)

Cukrkávalimonáda Achingly cute cafe with Renaissance-era painted roof beams. (p52)

Mistral Café Possibly the coolest bistro in the Old Town. (p67)

Bakeshop Praha A stylish bakery near the Jewish Quarter. (p65)

Best
Art

The city's holdings of fine art were pilfered over the centuries through wars and occupations, and museums here, while boasting occasional masterworks, lack the depth of galleries in Vienna and Paris. That said, the National Gallery's collections are strong in medieval art, baroque, and early modern surrealist and constructivist trends of the 20th century, when Czech artists came into their own.

LONELY PLANET/GETTY IMAGES ©

The Underappreciated Alfons Mucha

Alfons Mucha (1860–1939) is probably the most famous visual artist to come out of the Czech lands, though because he attained his fame in Paris, and not in Prague, his reputation remains more exalted abroad than at home. Mucha is best known for his posters of French actress Sarah Bernhardt, but he was a prolific artist whose work is featured at St Vitus Cathedral (p30) and the Municipal House (p79).

Best Art Museums

Veletržní Palác National Gallery's jaw-dropping collection of art from the 20th and 21st centuries. (p126)

Šternberg Palace National Gallery's collection of European art includes works by Goya and Rembrandt. (p36)

Mucha Museum Sensuous art nouveau posters, paintings and decorative panels of Alfons Mucha. (p95)

Convent of St Agnes Collection of medieval and early-Renaissance art is a treasure house of glowing Gothic altar paintings. (p65)

Best Public Art

Miminka (Mummy) Ten creepy babies crawling atop the Žižkov TV Tower, by David Černý. (p118)

Proudy David Černý sculpture features two guys relieving themselves into a puddle shaped like the Czech Republic. (p45)

Franz Kafka Monument This unusual sculpture has a mini-Franz sitting piggyback on his own headless body. (p65)

Cubist Lamp Post The world's one and only. (p97)

Best
Museums

Prague has tons of museums, big and small, scattered around the city, and they make for great rainy-day options. Most museums cater to specific interests, but alas, many of the collections are of the old-school variety: static objects displayed behind thick glass. The recently refurbished, interactive and loads-of-fun National Technical Museum is a welcome exception and great for kids.

JOHN BORTHWICK/GETTY IMAGES ©

Prague Jewish Museum
Displays the development of centuries of Jewish life and traditions with exhibitions in around half a dozen surviving synagogues. The highlight of the experience is to walk through the evocative former **Jewish cemetery**, with its thousands of jagged-edged tombstones. (p60, p62)

Karel Zeman Museum
Fascinating museum dedicated to a Czech film director who pioneered the art of special effects in movies. (p48)

National Technical Museum
The Czech Republic's industrial heritage is on riotous display,

with interactive exhibits and giant locomotives. (p129)

Franz Kafka Museum
Hard-core fans will delight in the writer's original documents and photos. (p49)

Miniature Museum
A delightfully quirky collection of miniature artwork, including the Lord's Prayer inscribed on a single strand of human hair. (p35)

Museum of Decorative Arts
A feast for the eyes, full of 16th- to 19th-century artefacts, such as furniture, tapestries, porcelain and glass. (p65)

☑ Top Tips

▶ Austerity measures have forced museums to cut back on admission-free days and other price reductions, but many places still offer discounted family tickets.

▶ Most museums restrict photography or levy a painfully high fee for the privilege; flash photography is nearly always banned.

▶ The **Prague City Card** (www.praguecitycard.com) offers free or discounted entry to around 50 sights, including many museums. Buy it at **Prague City Tourism** (www.prague.eu) offices.

Best
History

Prague history reads like a long novel, chock-full of characters who ride the city's fortunes from the heights of the Holy Roman Empire to the depths of the Eastern bloc. Fortunately, the city was spared mass destruction in WWII, and it's all on full display. From the castle, to the churches, to the corner shop, every building has a story.

Royal Heyday

Modern Prague draws its origins from the 7th century, when Princess Libuše is said to have stood at Vyšehrad Citadel and predicted a great city would someday arise. That great city became reality in the 14th century, when Emperor Charles IV made Prague the seat of the Holy Roman Empire. Religious conflicts between Hussites and Catholics reduced the kingdom to rubble, but another enlightened royal, Habsburg ruler Rudolf II, moved the seat of his vast empire to Prague Castle again in the 16th century. The good times were dashed once more, though, in another bout of religious conflict in the 17th century.

Czech National Revival

Prague languished under Habsburg occupation through the 17th and 18th centuries, until the forces of industrialisation weakened the grip of the Austrian royal family. Suddenly, there was a new class of educated Czechs agitating for cultural, linguistic and ultimately political freedoms. The Czechs' chance came in 1918, with the end of WWI and the fall of the Habsburg monarchy. That year saw the emergence of a new nation, Czechoslovakia, which did great things in the 1920s...until the Great Depression and Nazi Germany came calling.

The Worst of Times, the Best of Times

Nazi Germany occupied Czechoslovakia in stages in 1938 and '39 in the run-up to WWII. Nazi repression was cruel and most of the country's Jewish population was tragically murdered in the Holocaust, but the city at least was spared wartime destruction. Relief at the end of the war was brief, however, as Czechoslovakia fell into the orbit of Soviet Russia. Communist rule was both brutal and inept (at one point, in 1968, the Soviet Union had to invade its own ally just to keep it in line). The regime collapsed in 1989 as communism fell across Eastern Europe. The 'Velvet Revolution' that year ushered in a new era of democracy.

Astronomical Clock (p74)

Best Royal Sights

Vyšehrad Citadel Where it all began – Prague's oldest fortification. (p110)

Prague Castle Seat of Czech power for a thousand years. (p24)

Astronomical Clock Ancient mechanical marvel that still chimes on the hour. (p75)

St Nicholas Church The height of Habsburg-inspired baroque splendour. (p47)

Best National Revivial

Municipal House Art nouveau apogee of art and national aspiration. (p96)

National Theatre Built to showcase emerging Czech music and drama. (p107)

Best for Modern History

National Memorial to the Heroes of the Heydrich Terror Site where seven Czechoslovak partisans took refuge from the Nazis – and met tragic ends – in 1942. (p106)

TV Tower Communist power at its most potent. (p118)

John Lennon Wall This graffiti-splattered memorial was repainted each time the secret police whitewashed over it. (p45)

Best
For Kids

Czechs are very family-oriented, so there are plenty of activities for children around the city. An increasing number of Prague restaurants cater specifically for children, with play areas and so on, and many offer a children's menu; even if they don't, they can usually provide smaller portions for a lower price.

Into the Fresh Air

A great outing for kids (and parents) is Prague Zoo, located north of the centre in Troja. In addition, there are several other patches of green around town where you can spread a blanket and let the kids run free, such as Stromovka. Petřín is a beautiful park on a hill where parents and kids alike can take a break from sightseeing, and climb up the Petřín Lookout Tower for terrific views over Prague.

☑ Top Tips

▶ Kids up to age 15 normally pay half-price for attractions (under six free)

▶ On public transport, kids from six to 15 pay half-price.

Best of the Outdoors

Stromovka Prague's largest central park, with lots of playgrounds. (p129)

Prague Zoo Aside from the animals, attractions include a miniature cable car. (p130)

Petřín Funicular Kids will get a thrill riding this funicular up to the top of the hill. (p43)

Slav Island Rent a paddle boat and enjoy a ride on the Vltava. (p105)

Best Indoor Activities

National Technical Museum A must-stop for inquisitive adolescents and their tech-savvy parents. (p129)

Miniature Museum Tiny exhibits and curiosities spark kids' imaginations at this delightful little museum. (p35)

Laterna Magika Kids love the optical illusions onstage during the 'Black Light' theatre performances here. (p108)

Mořský Svět Prague's 'Sea World', at the Výstaviště exhibition grounds, boasts big aquariums and lots of aquatic life. (p129)

RICHARD NEBESKY/ROBERT HARDING/GETTY IMAGES ©

 Best
For Free

Once a famously inexpensive destination, Prague is no longer cheap – there's not much on offer without a price attached. That said, in a city as beautiful as Prague, you don't need to spend lots of time (or money) on pricey museums. The parks and gardens, including the hilltop vista from Letná Gardens, are free, as is the street entertainment on Charles Bridge.

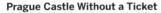

Prague Castle Without a Ticket

Admission to the interiors of Prague Castle, including St Vitus Cathedral, is hefty. But many people don't realize that the castle grounds, including the surrounding gardens, are free to roam at your leisure. The highlights of a visit here are the views over Malá Strana and the hourly changing of the guard; the most elaborate show is performed daily at noon.

Best Free Sights

Petřín Hill Entrance to the park is gratis; skip the funicular and just hike up. (p42)

Astronomical Clock The hourly chiming is public and free. (p75)

Vyšehrad Cemetery The beautiful cemetery is the final resting place

for composers Smetana and Dvořák, as well as art nouveau artist Alfons Mucha. (p111)

Letná Gardens The sweeping views are free; beers from the beer garden cost extra. (p129)

☑ Top Tips

▶ Ask at tourist-information offices about free concerts, theatrical performances and cultural events happening during your visit.

▶ Visits to most churches (except St Vitus Cathedral and St Nicholas Church in Malá Strana) are free.

▶ Although you'll have to pay for a guided tour of the Municipal House (p96), you can wander through the glorious art nouveau cafe and to the downstairs American Bar without a ticket.

Best
Architecture

Prague is an open-air museum of architecture; most of the centre is protected as a Unesco World Heritage listing. Prague's architectural heritage was built up over the centuries, with the earliest buildings in the Romanesque and Gothic styles dating back nearly a thousand years. Later styles were added over time as fashions changed.

The Style of Bohemian Kings

Romanesque and Gothic are the oldest architectural styles surviving in Prague and are associated with the early centuries of the Bohemian kingdom. Romanesque is identified by rounded facades and massive walls, and is best seen in the handful of circular churches (rotundas) still standing. Gothic is Prague's signature style, characterised by tall, pointed arches, ribbed vaults, external flying buttresses, and narrow windows.

Baroque Razzle Dazzle

When the Habsburgs assumed the Bohemian throne in the early 16th century, they invited Italian architects to Prague to help create a royal city worthy of their status. With Renaissance style, the Italians brought a new enthusiasm for classical forms and an obsession with symmetry. Highly ornate baroque came a century later: it was used by the Catholic Church to dazzle – and woo – the sceptical locals.

Arrival of Art Nouveau

By the 19th century, architects, seemingly, had run out of ideas and consciously imitated historical styles like Gothic and Renaissance, often appending a 'neo' to the front (hence 'neo-Gothic'). By the end of the century, art nouveau blew this pomposity away in an orgy of beauty.

GUILLERMO MURCIA/GETTY IMAGES ©

☑ **Top Tips**

▶ For more on Prague architecture, take a specialised tour such as Thousand Years of Prague Architecture (see www.walkingtours. cz).

▶ *Prague: An Architectural Guide* is a photographic encyclopaedia by Mark Smith, Michal Schonberg and Radomira Sedlakova.

Dancing Building (p105), Nové Město

Best Romanesque & Gothic

Rotunda of St Martin Tiny, circular church in Vyšehrad is reputedly Prague's oldest standing building and a perfect example of Romanesque architecture. (p111)

St Vitus Cathedral Gothic to the tips of its famous spires. (p96)

Charles Bridge Prague's most famous bridge is a Gothic landmark. (p76)

Best Renaissance & Baroque

St Nicholas Church In Malá Strana, the mother of all baroque churches in Prague. (p47)

Loreta The pilgrimage site is modelled after the Italian original. (p32)

Best National Revival & Art Nouveau

Municipal House Glittering art nouveau in top form. (p96)

Grand Hotel Evropa Fading grandeur at this ornate art nouveau hotel and cafe. (p93)

Best Modern Architecture

Dancing Building The shape of the building mimics a dancing couple. (p105)

Veletržní Palác This mammoth functionalist structure from the 1920s doesn't look like your everyday palace. (p126)

Best
Shopping

Although the streets are lined with stores, Prague doesn't initially seem a particularly inspiring shopping destination. But if you know where to look, you can find above-average versions of classic Czech souvenirs: Bohemian crystal and glassware, garnet and amber jewellery, and wooden marionettes. Think outside the box: Czech liquor, farm-produced beauty products and old-school children's toys all make great gifts.

For mainstream shopping, central Na Příkopě boasts international chains from H&M to Zara. For the most part, you can put your wallet away along Wenceslas Square (not a bad idea anyway, considering the pickpocketing that goes on here). Instead, explore the Old Town's winding alleyways. Ritzy Pařížská is often called Prague's Champs Élysées and is lined with luxury brands like Cartier, Dolce & Gabbana, Hugo Boss and Ferragamo. Dlouhá, Dušní and surrounding streets house some original fashion boutiques, while even central Celetná contains a worthwhile stop or two.

TRAVEL INK/GETTY IMAGES ©

jewellery, posters and books. (p88)

Moser Ornate Bohemian glass objects. (p101)

Artěl Traditional glass-making meets modern design in this stylish shop in Malá Strana. (p55)

Best for Unique Souvenirs

Botanicus Rustic-chic beauty products from this popular old apothecary. (p86)

Manufaktura Specialises in Czech traditional crafts and wooden toys. (p88)

Art Deco Galerie Czech antiques galore; hunt for treasures here on a rainy day. (p86)

Best for Design & Glass

Modernista Czech cubist and art deco design with cool ceramics,

Best for Books & Toys

Marionety Truhlář In Malá Strana, quirky shop stocks traditional marionettes from workshops around the Czech Republic. (p55)

Shakespeare & Sons More than just a bookshop – a congenial literary hang-out. (p55)

Houpací Kůň (Rocking Horse Toy Shop) Shop for high-quality, traditional Czech toys. (p39)

Best Clubs

ELAN FLEISHER/GETTY IMAGES ©

No one comes to Prague specifically for cutting-edge clubbing, and the scene pales in comparison to nearby Berlin. While there are plenty of places to go dancing and big-name DJs do occasionally put in an appearance here, Prague is not the place for chasing the latest trends. Instead, it's a destination for letting your hair down and not taking things too seriously.

Musically, dance clubs have a penchant for 1980s and '90s pop; locals reckon the predilection for '80s tunes in particular is a rose-tinted, if slightly ironic, nostalgia for the simpler, more controlled days of communism. Prague also has many basement music clubs, DJ bars and edgy 'experimental' venues. If you're serious about clubbing, do as the locals do and head to Holešovice, where many of the city's most active nightlife spots are clustered.

☑ Top Tips

▶ Go late. The dance floors are rarely ever populated before midnight.

▶ There's usually no dress code – aside from short pants, you can wear what you want.

▶ Check the clubs' listings ahead of time to find out about DJ line-ups and themed nights.

Best Upscale Nightclubs

Mecca A slice of Ibiza in the northern Prague suburb of Holešovice. (p132)

SaSaZu A 'superclub' in Holešovice where international DJs play in a UFO-styled booth. (p132)

Radost FX Chilled-out, bohemian atmosphere in Vinohrady, with themed dance parties each night of the week. (p123)

Best for Unpretentious Fun

Lucerna Music Bar The venue for weekend '80s- and '90s-themed dance nights. (p100)

Techtle Mechtle A popular cellar dance bar on Vinohrady's main drag. (p123)

Hospoda U Buldoka The after-hours dancing gets fast and furious at this crowded Smíchov pub. (p57)

Best
Live Music

Prague is a great destination for live music, particularly for classical concerts and opera but also for jazz, blues and rock. The classical season runs from September through May, and on nearly any night of the week, you'll have half a dozen options to choose from. Jazz venues tend to focus on local talent, but clubs do occasionally feature big names from abroad.

DANITA DELIMONT/GETTY IMAGES ©

Opera & Classical Music

Prague has a long, proud tradition of opera and classical music. In the 18th century, Mozart chose to premiere his opera *Don Giovanni* here rather than in Vienna, saying 'my Praguers understand me'. In the 19th century, the city was the stomping ground for major European composers like Antonín Dvořák and Bedřich Smetana. These days, the city is home to some lovely old theatres.

Jazz

Czechs figured prominently in European jazz circles from the 1920s until the 1948 communist coup d'état, and even under communism the style survived in some form. Prague's first professional jazz club, Reduta, opened during the less censorial atmosphere of the 1960s.

Rock & Pop

Rock has a long tradition of dissent here, going back to the '80s, when underground bands were a bedrock of anticommunism. These days, music is less political but more energetic, and the scene is as fragmented and diverse as anywhere else: the hip-hop, electronic, indie and metal genres are all thriving. Stadium concerts pile through town all summer long.

☑ **Top Tips**

▸ Plan ahead and book seats in advance. Big performances sell out.

▸ Venue websites are a great place to see what's on during your stay. You can buy tickets online.

▸ Dress up for classical concerts and opera. This is one night to leave the jeans in the hotel room.

LONELY PLANET/GETTY IMAGES ©

Jazz Club U Staré Paní (p86)

Best Classical Venues

National Theatre Spectacular venue for traditional opera, drama and ballet. (p107)

Prague State Opera Impressive neo-rococo building makes a glorious setting for opera and ballet. (p100)

Estates Theatre Oldest theatre in Prague, famed as the place where Mozart conducted the premiere of *Don Giovanni* in 1787. (p85)

Dvořák Hall Home to the world-renowned Czech Philharmonic Orchestra. (p70)

Best for Jazz & Blues

Jazz Republic Stages all kinds of live music, including rock and fusion as well as jazz. (p108)

AghaRTA Jazz Centrum Hosts gigs by leading international artists. (p86)

Blues Sklep Old Town basement provides atmospheric setting for nightly jazz sessions. (p86)

Jazz Club U Staré Paní Varied program of modern jazz, soul, blues and Latin rhythms. (p86)

Jazz Dock Riverside locale mixes blues with views. (p57)

Best Alternative

Malostranská beseda Pleasing mix of old-school Czech rockers and up-and-coming acts. (p55)

Palác Akropolis A long-standing Prague institution, host to all kinds of live music. (p123)

Cross Club The ultimate in Prague's 'industrial' clubs, packed with mechanical gadgetry. (p132)

Roxy The queen of the city's experimental scene, mixing art, music and live performance. (p70)

Best
Gay & Lesbian

LONELY PLANET/GETTY IMAGES ©

Prague has a small but lively gay and lesbian scene, with most of the action concentrated in the neighbourhood of Vinohrady, just outside of the centre. Homosexuality is widely tolerated and gay couples are not likely to experience any overt discrimination. The annual Prague Pride march (www.praguepride.cz), usually held in August, is the largest of its kind in Central Europe.

According to one regular, the scene is easygoing. There's little in the way of 'face control' or dress codes at the door, and even the top venues usually don't charge entrance fees. Also, there aren't many problems with rampaging British stag parties, which are fewer these days, and generally stick to the centre in any case. Most gay clubs are welcoming to both gay men and lesbians.

Best Gay Bars & Clubs

Termix Industrial-style bar in Vinohrady with a small but happening dance floor. (p123)

Saints British-run gay bar in Vinohrady is laid-back and friendly. (p122)

Radost FX Popular, mixed gay and straight dance club with a chilled-out, bohemian atmosphere. (p123)

Cafe Celebrity Part of a cluster of gay-friendly places that make up the old Radio Palác building in the heart of Vinohrady. (p122)

☑ Top Tips

▶ Dress neat but casual – as elsewhere in Prague, the dress code is laid-back.

▶ Although things differ from bar to bar, the scene is mixed between Czechs and foreigners.

▶ An excellent first stop is Saints, which runs a gay travel and accommodation service and maintains an up-to-date website with an interactive map of the scene.

▶ A useful website is **Gay Guide Prague** (http://prague.gayguide. net).

Survival Guide

Survival Guide

Before You Go

When to Go

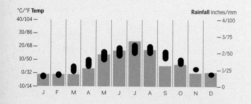

⇒ Spring (Apr–Jun)
April is the start of
the tourist season.
Trees bud in mid-April.
Accommodation tightens
at Easter and for the
Prague Spring music
festival in May.

⇒ Summer (Jul–Aug)
Sunny and occasionally
hot. All attractions open.

⇒ Autumn (Sep–Oct)
Often sunny but cool.
Some attractions close
on 1 October for winter.

⇒ Winter (Nov–Mar)
Short, dark days, snow
and occasionally blustery
winds. Tourists descend
for lively Christmas and
New Year festivities.

Book Your Stay

⇒ Air-conditioning isn't
necessary most of the
year; the exception is July
and August, when Prague
is prone to an occasional
heatwave.

⇒ Parking can be very
tight. If driving, work out
parking details with the
hotel in advance and avoid
hotels in Malá Strana and
the Old Town.

⇒ To save money, consider
booking a private single or
double in a hostel. Many
are very nice and offer
excellent value.

⇒ If noise is an issue, ask
for a room away from the
street. Bear in mind that
top-floor rooms, below the
roof, can be hot and airless
in summer.

⇒ You can often find
last-minute bargains for
the top-end hotels on the
standard online booking
sites.

⇒ Malá Strana is a par-
ticularly scenic location

in which to stay, but it's worth considering a room in one of Prague's inner suburbs like Vinohrady, Smíchov or Holešovice, as central Prague is easily reached by public transport.

Useful Websites

Hotels Prague (www.hotelsprague.cz) Listings of the city's best historic hotels and B&Bs.

Guide Prague (www.guideprague.com) Well-run booking site that offers plenty of photos.

Booking.com (www.booking.com) Helps you make reservations at hundreds of Prague hotels.

Lonely Planet (www.lonelyplanet.com) Author-recommended reviews and online booking.

Best Budget

Fusion Hotel (www.fusionhotels.com) It's a hostel, it's a hotel, it's designer heaven...

Holiday Home (www.holidayhome.cz) Popular, family-owned pension in a quiet neighbourhood.

Mosaic House (www.mosaichouse.com) A blend of four-star hotel and boutique hostel with designer details.

Czech Inn (www.czech-inn.com) Great value and atmosphere in an up-and-coming neighbourhood.

Best Midrange

Domus Henrici (www.domus-henrici.cz) Peaceful seclusion just a short stroll from the castle.

Lokál Inn (www.lokalinn.cz) Lovely baroque setting with excellent restaurant close to Charles Bridge.

Hunger Wall Residence (www.hungerwall.eu) Spotlessly clean and modernised short-stay apartments.

Dům u velké boty (www.dumuvelkeboty.cz) Lovely old pension set on a quiet square.

Best Top End

Golden Well Hotel (www.goldenwell.cz) Historic, luxury hotel in the ultimate location – beneath the castle walls.

Savic Hotel (www.savic.eu) Housed in a former monastery, this hotel is bursting with character.

Icon Hotel (www.iconhotel.eu) Cutting-edge designer hotel that's a hang-out for Prague's beautiful people.

Le Palais (www.vi-hotels.com/en/le-palais) Luxury hotel housed in a gorgeous belle époque building.

Best Short-Stay Apartments

Happy House Rentals (www.happyhouserentals.com) Specialises in short- and long-term rental apartments.

Mary's Travel & Tourist Service (www.marys.cz) Friendly, efficient agency offering private rooms, hostels, pensions, apartments and hotels in Prague and surrounding areas.

Prague Apartments (www.prague-apartment.com) Web-based service with comfortable, IKEA-furnished flats. Availability of apartments shown online.

Stop City (www.stopcity.com) Specialises in apartments, private rooms and pensions in the city centre, Vinohrady and Žižkov areas.

Arriving in Prague

☑ **Top Tip** For the best way to get to your accommodation, see p17.

Václav Havel Airport Prague

This international **airport** (www.prg.aero) is 17km west of the city centre.

➡ **Cedaz Shuttlebus** (www.cedaz.cz) Mini shuttle-buses take travellers to and from the airport to its station near náměstí Republiky. Daily shuttles leave from both locations every 30 minutes between 7.30am and 7pm; one-way tickets cost 150Kč.

➡ **Airport Express (AE) Bus** Runs between the airport and Prague's main train station at 30-minute intervals. Service starts at 5am and the last bus leaves around 9.30pm. Buy your ticket from the driver for 60Kč.

➡ **AAA Radio Taxi** (www.aaataxi.cz) Prague's most reliable taxi service. To book a taxi inside the airport, look for the AAA desk in the arrivals hall. A ride to náměstí Republiky will cost about 600Kč.

➡ **Bus 119** Catch the city bus from the airport to the closest metro station, Dejvická, on one end of Line A. Standard transport fares apply; the current fare for a 90-minute window of time is adult/concession 32/16Kč. If you're toting sizeable luggage, you'll need to pay an extra 16Kč to bring it on the bus.

Prague Main Train Station

Nearly all international trains arrive at Prague's main station, **Praha hlavní nádraží** (www.cd.cz; Wilsonova 8, Nové Město).

➡ To Old Town, take metro Line C to Muzeum and change to Line A to Staroměstská station.

➡ To get to Prague Castle, take metro Line C to Muzeum and change to Line A to Hradčanská station or Malostranská station.

➡ To get to Wenceslas Square, just walk 5 minutes (it's two blocks away).

Note that some trains arrive at Prague's other large train station, **Praha-Holešovice** (www.cd.cz; Vrbenského, Holešovice), conveniently connected to the Nádraži Holešovice station on the metro's Line C.

Florenc Bus Station

Nearly all international buses use the renovated **Florenc bus station** (www.florenc.cz; Křižíkova 4, Karlín). The bus station is accessible by both the metro's B and C lines. To get to the Old Town from Florenc, take Line B to Náměstí Republiky. To reach Wenceslas Square (and Old Town), take Line B to Můstek. At Můstek, you can change to Line A to continue onto Malá Strana or Prague Castle (Malostranská station). Line C goes to the main train station (Praha hlavní nádraží).

Getting Around

Prague has an excellent integrated public-transport system (www.dpp.cz) of metro, trams, buses and night trams, but when you're moving around the compact Old Town or the castle area, it will be more convenient – and scenic – to use your feet. If you're using the metro system, bank on about one or two minutes per metro stop. Times between tram stops are posted at each stop and on www.dpp.cz.

Metro

☑ **Best for...** Quick transportation between major sights, connecting to the train station and venturing outside the tourist areas.

➡ The metro operates from 5am to midnight.

➡ There are three lines: Line A (green) runs from Dejvická in the northwest to Depo Hostivař in the east; Line B (yellow) runs from Zličín in the southwest to Černý Most in the northeast; and Line C (red) runs from Háje in the southeast to Letňany in the north.

➡ Services are fast and frequent. You'll find a map in every metro station and metro train. The nearest metro station is noted after the Ⓜ in listings.

➡ You must buy a *jízdenka* (ticket) before boarding, and then validate it by punching it in the little yellow machine in the metro-station lobby or on the bus or tram when you begin your journey. Checks by inspectors are frequent; they'll fine you

Tickets & Passes

Tickets are interchangeable on all metros, trams and buses. Buy tickets at metro stations or nearby news-stands – but never from the driver. If you're staying longer than a few hours, it's easier to buy a one-day or three-day pass than dealing with individual tickets.

➡ **Basic ticket** Valid for 90 minutes; adult/concession 32/16Kč.

➡ **Short-term ticket** Valid for 30 minutes; adult/concession 24/12Kč.

➡ **One-day ticket** Valid for 24 hours; adult/concession 110/55Kč.

➡ **Three-day ticket** Valid for 72 hours; 310Kč for all ages.

➡ **Luggage ticket** Needed for large pieces; 16Kč.

for travelling without a time-stamped ticket (the fine is reduced if you pay on the spot).

➡ You'll need coins for ticket machines at metro stations and major tram stops. You can also buy tickets at news-stands, some hotels, tourist-information offices and metro-station ticket offices.

Tram & Bus

☑ **Best for...** Scenic rides, connecting to attractions far off the metro lines, and for travellers who can't easily walk from point A to B. Most visitors won't have any reason to

get on a bus, but a tram ride is a classic Prague experience.

➡ Important tram lines to remember are 22 (runs to Prague Castle, Malá Strana and Charles Bridge), 17 and 18 (run to the Jewish Quarter and Old Town Sq) and 11 (runs to Žižkov and Vinohrady).

➡ Regular tram and bus services operate from 5am to midnight (see www.dpp.cz for maps and timetables). After this, night trams (51 to 58) and buses (501 to 512) still rumble across the city about every 40 minutes.

→ Night trams intersect at Lazarská in Nové Město. If you're planning a late evening, find out if one of these services passes near where you're staying.

→ Be aware that few tram or bus stops sell tickets. So if you're using single tickets, buy several in the metro station or at newspaper stands, then save a couple of unstamped ones for later and validate them upon boarding.

Taxi

☑ **Best for**... Late-night rides back to the hotel, airport transfers, and when you're running late for a show at the National Theatre.

→ For years, Prague's taxi drivers were renowned for scams – huge fines and crackdowns have made a big difference, however. Most drivers now turn on their meters when picking up a fare, as legally required. If a driver won't comply, find another taxi.

→ Look for the 'Taxi Fair Place' scheme, which provides authorised taxis in key tourist areas. Drivers can charge a maximum fare and must announce the estimated price in advance.

→ Away from official 'Taxi Fair Place' stands, the streets around Wenceslas Sq, Národní třída, Na Příkopě, Praha hlavní nádraží, Old Town Sq and Malostranské náměstí are the most notorious rip-off spots. Make sure to ask the fare in advance to avoid being taken for a ride (so to speak).

→ In the city centre, trips should be around 150Kč to 200Kč, a trip to the suburbs no more than 450Kč, and to the airport around 600Kč to 700Kč.

In our experience, the following radio-taxi services are all reliable and honest:

AAA Radio Taxi (📞14014, 222 333 222; www.aaataxi.cz)

Halo Taxi (📞244 114 411; www.halotaxi.cz)

ProfiTaxi (📞14015; www. profitaxi.cz)

Bicycle

☑ **Best for**... Sightseeing and green travellers.

Despite cobblestones, hills and gigantic tour buses, in recent years Prague has become more bike friendly. For rentals, try these outfitters (except in winter, when they're closed):

Praha Bike (📞732 388 880; www.prahabike.cz; Dlouhá 24, Staré Město; rental per day 550Kč, tours per person starting at 540Kč; 🕓9am-8pm; Ⓜ Náměstí Republiky) Rentals and guided tours in Old Town. Has tandem bikes and can deliver for an extra fee.

City Bike Prague (📞776 180 284; www.citybike-prague. com; Královská 5, Staré Město; rental per day 500Kč, tours per person 550-800Kč; 🕓9am-7pm Apr-Oct; Ⓜ Náměstí Republiky) Also in Old Town, City Bike has a great selection of wheels.

Biko Adventures Prague (📞733 750 990; www.bikoadventures.com; Vratislavova 3, Nové Město; standard rental per day 450Kč, group tours per person from 1250Kč; 🕓9am-6pm Apr-Oct; 🚋7, 17 to Výtoň) Rents bikes and offers day-long guided trips for riders of all levels.

Essential Information

Business Hours

☑ **Top Tip** Avid shoppers should note that local stores (those not specifically geared to tourists) often close on Sunday.

Banks 8am to 4.30pm Monday to Friday

Bars 11am to midnight or later

Main post office (Jindřišská 14, Nové Město) 2am to midnight

Shops 8.30am to 8pm Monday to Friday, to 6pm Saturday and Sunday

Restaurants 10am to 11pm, though kitchens often close by 10pm

Electricity

230V/50Hz

Emergency

EU-wide emergency hotline (☎112)

Fire (☎150)

Municipal Police (☎156)

State Police (☎158)

Money

☑ **Top Tip** Watch for rip-offs at private exchange booths. These often lure tourists with attractive-looking exchange rates, which turn out to be only available when changing large sums.

➡ Credit cards are widely accepted.

➡ The Czech crown (Koruna česká, or Kč) is divided into 100 hellers (h), though these tiny coins no longer circulate. Prices are sometimes denominated in fractions of crowns. In these instances, the total is rounded to the nearest whole crown.

➡ Keep small change handy for public toilets and tram-ticket machines, and always try to keep some small notes for shops, cafes and bars.

Public Holidays

Banks, department stores and some shops will be closed on public holidays. Restaurants, museums and tourist attractions tend to stay open.

New Year's Day 1 January

Easter Monday March/April

Labour Day 1 May

Liberation Day 8 May

Sts Cyril & Methodius Day 5 July

Jan Hus Day 6 July

Czech Statehood Day 28 September

Republic Day 28 October

Struggle for Freedom & Democracy Day 17 November

Christmas Eve (Generous Day) 24 December

Christmas Day 25 December

St Stephen's Day 26 December

Tipping
Tip 10% of the tab in restaurants or bars to reward good service, though look carefully to see that the tip hasn't already been added (an annoying practice you might find at touristy places). Taxi drivers won't expect a tip, but you can round up a few crowns if the driver has been helpful.

Money-Saving Tips

➡ Forget taxis – take a shuttle bus from the airport to the city, then walk or use public transport.

➡ Skip the sushi and eat Czech food; you'll find the best value for your crowns in pubs. Look for set-lunch specials.

➡ At restaurants, portions are large and normally come with sides, so you can skip the starters. Local beer is much cheaper than wine (and delicious).

➡ Don't exchange cash at the airport. Instead, withdraw local currency with your ATM card.

➡ Don't worry about missing museums if cash is tight – Prague is best explored outdoors and on foot.

➡ When going to the theatre, you can get cheaper tickets for around 100Kč.

Safe Travel

Prague is a low-crime city and you're not likely to experience serious problems. Pickpocketing and petty theft, however, remain rife, especially around the main tourist attractions. Keep valuables well out of reach and be alert in crowds and on public transport. If you are the victim of a pickpocket, report the crime as soon as possible at any nearby police station. Remember to retain any paperwork you might need for insurance purposes.

For lost or stolen passports, embassies can normally issue travel documents on the spot.

Telephone

☑ **Top Tip** If your mobile or cellphone is unlocked, you can buy a prepaid SIM card, available from any mobile-phone shop for around 450Kč (including 300Kč of calling credit), to make local calls at cheaper local rates (though you can't use your existing mobile number).

➡ The Czech Republic uses GSM 900, compatible with mobile phones from the rest of Europe, Australia and New Zealand (but not with North American or Japanese phones).

➡ Some North Americans, however, have dual-band GSM 1900/900 phones that do work here;

check with your service provider.

Country & City Codes

The country code for the Czech Republic is 420; there are no area codes inside the country.

All phone numbers have nine digits, which must be always dialled whether calling next door or a distant town. All landline numbers in Prague begin with a 2; mobile numbers begin with a 6 or 7.

Using Your Smartphone

If you plan on using a 'smartphone' like an iPhone or Android device, it's best to contact your home provider to consider short-term international calling and data plans appropriate to what you might need.

Smartphones can still be used as handy wi-fi devices, even without a special plan. Be sure to switch your phone to 'airplane' mode on arrival, which blocks out calls and text messages. Also, turn off your phone's 'data roaming' setting to avoid unwanted roaming fees.

Tourist Information

The official provider of tourist information is **Prague City Tourism** (formerly Prague Welcome). Its offices are good sources of maps and general information, as well as an excellent resource for finding what's on during your stay. Its main website (www.prague.eu) has extensive information in English.

Prague City Tourism – Airport (⏲8am-8pm)

Prague City Tourism – Malá Strana (Map p46; Malá Strana Bridge Tower, Mostecká; ⏲10am-6pm Apr-Oct)

Prague City Tourism – Old Town Hall (Map p78; Staroměstské náměstí 5; ⏲9am-7pm)

Prague City Tourism – Rytířská (Map p78; Rytířská 31, Staré Město; ⏲10am-6pm)

Language

Czech belongs to the western branch of the Slavic language family. Many travellers flinch when they see written Czech, but pronouncing it is not as hard as it may seem at first. Most of the sounds in Czech are also found in English, and of the few that aren't, only one can be a little tricky to master – *rzh* (written as ř). Also, Czech letters always have the same pronunciation, so you'll become familiar with their pronunciation really quickly.

With a little practice and reading our pronunciation guides as if they were English, you'll be understood. Just make sure you always stress the first syllable of a word – in italics in this chapter – and pronounce any vowel written with an accent mark over it as a long sound. In this chapter (m/f) indicates masculine and feminine forms.

To enhance your trip with a phrasebook, visit **lonelyplanet.com**. Lonely Planet iPhone phrasebooks are available through the Apple App store.

Basics

Hello.
Ahoj. uh·hoy

Goodbye.
Na shledanou. nuh·skhle·duh·noh

Excuse me.
Promiňte. pro·min'·te

Sorry.
Promiňte. pro·min'·te

Please.
Prosím. pro·seem

Thank you.
Děkuji. dye·ku·yi

Yes./No.
Ano./Ne. uh·no/ne

Do you speak English?
Mluvíte mlu·vee·te
anglicky? uhn·glits·ki

I don't understand.
Nerozumím. ne·ro·zu·meem

Eating & Drinking

I'm a vegetarian. (m/f)
Jsem vegetarián/ ysem ve·ge·tuh·ri·an/
vegetariánka. ve·ge·tuh·ri·an·ka

Cheers!
Na zdraví! nuh zdruh·vee

That was delicious!
To bylo lahodné! to bi·lo luh·hod·nair

Please bring the bill.
Prosím pro·seem
přineste účet. przhi·nes·te oo·chet

I'd like ... , please. (m/f)
Chtěl/Chtěla khtyel/khtye·luh
bych ..., prosím. bikh ... pro·seem

a table	*stůl*	stool
for (two)	*pro (dva)*	pro (dvuh)
that dish	*ten pokrm*	ten po·krm
the drinks list	*nápojový lístek*	na·po·yo·vee lees·tek

Shopping

I'm looking for ...
Hledám ... hle·dam ...

How much is it?
Kolik to stojí? ko·lik to sto·yee

That's too expensive.
To je moc drahé. to ye mots druh·hair

Can you lower the price?
Můžete mi   moo·zhe·te mi
snížit cenu?   snyee·zhit tse·nu

Emergencies

Help!
Pomoc!   po·mots

Call a doctor!
Zavolejte   zuh·vo·ley·te
lékaře!   lair·kuh·rzhe

Call the police!
Zavolejte   zuh·vo·ley·te
policii!   po·li·tsi·yi

I'm lost. (m/f)
Zabloudil/   zuh·bloh·dyil/
Zabloudila   zuh·bloh·dyi·luh
jsem.   ysem

I'm ill. (m/f)
Jsem nemocný/   ysem ne·mots·nee/
nemocná.   ne·mots·na

Where are the toilets?
Kde jsou toalety?   gde ysoh to·uh·le·ti

Time & Numbers

What time is it?
Kolik je hodin?   ko·lik ye ho·dyin

It's (10) o'clock.
Je jedna   ye yed·nuh
hodina.   ho·dyi·nuh

At what time?
V kolik hodin?   f ko·lik ho·dyin

morning	ráno	ra·no
afternoon	odpoledne	ot·po·led·ne
evening	večer	ve·cher
yesterday	včera	fche·ruh
today	dnes	dnes
tomorrow	zítra	zee·truh

1	jeden	ye·den
2	dva	dvuh
3	tři	trzhi
4	čtyři	chti·rzhi
5	pět	pyet
6	šest	shest
7	sedm	se·dm
8	osm	o·sm
9	devět	de·vyet
10	deset	de·set

Transport & Directions

Where's the ...?
Kde je ...?   gde ye ...

What's the address?
Jaká je   yuh·ka ye
adresa?   uh·dre·suh

Can you show me (on the map)?
Můžete   moo·zhe·te
mi to ukázat   mi to u·ka·zuht
(na mapě)?   (nuh muh·pye)

A ticket to ..., please.
Jízdenku   yeez·den·ku
do ..., prosim.   do ... pro·seem

What time does the bus/train leave?
V kolik hodin   f ko·lik ho·dyin
odjíždí   od·yeezh·dyee
autobus/vlak?   ow·to·bus/vluhk

Please stop here.
Prosím vás   pro·seem vas
zastavte.   zuhs·tuhf·te

I'd like a taxi.
Potřebuji   po·trzhe·bu·yi
taxíka.   tuhk·see·kuh

Is this taxi available?
Je tento taxík   ye ten·to tuhk·seek
volný?   vol·nee

Behind the Scenes

Send Us Your Feedback

We love to hear from travellers – your comments help make our books better. We read every word, and we guarantee that your feedback goes straight to the authors. Visit **lonelyplanet.com/contact** to submit your updates and suggestions.

Note: We may edit, reproduce and incorporate your comments in Lonely Planet products such as guidebooks, websites and digital products, so let us know if you don't want your comments reproduced or your name acknowledged. For a copy of our privacy policy visit lonelyplanet.com/privacy.

Our Readers

Many thanks to the travellers who wrote to us with useful advice and anecdotes:

Charles Carayon, Geoffrey Cox, Luis Figueira, Jonathan Franklin, Alana Goldman, Marie Hardel, Maureen Harrington, Vera Lanängen, Ian Parker, Lisanne Peschier, John Shearer, Petr Vůjtěch, Jude Wells, Jean Yang.

Mark's Thanks

I would like to thank my friends here in Prague for constantly suggesting great places for inclusion in this guide.

Kateřina Pavlitová, marketing director at Prague City Tourism, was always willing to help out with information and enthusiasm. Lonely Planet Prague author Neil Wilson helped to find many of the great restaurants and bars included here.

Acknowledgments

Cover photograph: Church of Our Lady Before Týn, Old Town Square, Francesco Iacobelli/AWL.

This Book

This 4th edition of *Pocket Prague* was written by Mark Baker. The previous edition was written by Bridget Gleeson. This book was commissioned in Lonely Planet's London office, and produced by the following:

Destination Editors Joe Bindloss, Gemma Graham **Product Editor** Martine Power **Senior Cartographers** Mark Griffiths, Valentina Kremenchutskaya **Book Designer** Clara Monitto **Assisting Editors** Ali Lemer, Charlotte Orr **Cover Researcher** Naomi Parker **Thanks to** Imogen Bannister, Sasha Baskett, Elin Berglund, Brendan Dempsey, Indra Kilfoyle, Claire Naylor, Karyn Noble, Katie O'Connell, Ellie Simpson, Angela Tinson, Tasmin Waby, Lauren Wellicome, Juan Winata

Index

Our Writer

Mark Baker

Prague resident Mark Baker first moved to the city in the early 1990s and has lived there, off and on, the better part of 20 years. He was a founder and co-owner of the Globe Bookstore & Café in Prague, and has worked as a journalist for the Economist Group, Bloomberg News and Radio Free Europe/Radio Liberty. In 2008 he began writing guidebooks for Lonely Planet. In addition to this edition of *Pocket Prague*, he's authored Lonely Planet's *Prague & the Czech Republic*, as well as Lonely Planet guides to Romania & Bulgaria, Poland, Slovenia and the Baltic countries.

Published by Lonely Planet Publications Pty Ltd
ABN 36 005 607 983
4th edition – Nov 2014
ISBN 978 1 74220 878 7
© Lonely Planet 2014 Photographs © as indicated 2014
10 9 8 7 6 5 4 3 2 1
Printed in China